Astrology
For Everyday Living

By Janet Harris

1976 EDITION

Published by
Melvin Powers
WILSHIRE BOOK COMPANY
12015 Sherman Road
No. Hollywood, California 91605
Telephone: (213) 875-1711

"What chariots, what horses
Against us shall bide,
While the stars in their courses
Do fight on our side."
                    "The Astrologer's Song"
                    —Rudyard Kipling

Printed by

HAL LEIGHTON PRINTING CO.
P.O. Box 1231
Beverly Hills, California 90213
Telephone: (213) 983-1105

Copyright © 1961 by

Bold Face Books, Inc.

Manufactured in the United States of America

Library of Congress Catalog Card No.: 61-15728

ISBN 0-87980-007-0

Contents

FIG. A

SIGNS OF THE ZODIAC

Reading clockwise:
A Vernal equinox:
   Aries, Taurus, Gemini.
B Summer solstice:
   Cancer, Leo, Virgo.
C Autumnal equinox:
   Libra, Scorpio, Sagittarius.
D Winter Solstice:
   Capricorn, Aquarius, Pisces.

FIG. B

SAMPLE HOROSCOPE
Birth Chart

Queen Elizabeth II
April 21, 1926
              1:40 A.M.

FIG. C

ASTROLOGICAL SYMBOLS
The Planets and Luminaries

⊙ Sun   ♂ Mars   ♅ Uranus
☽ Moon   ♃ Jupiter   ♆ Neptune
☿ Mercury   ♄ Saturn   ♇ Pluto
♀ Venus

The Aspects

Favorable Aspects: Trine, △ , Sextile ✳ , Semi-Sextile ⌵ , Adverse
Aspects: Opposition ☍ , Square □ , Semi-Square ∠ , Quincunx ⚹ .
Aspects whose influences vary according to the Planets involved:
Conjunction ☌ , Parallel P.

Glossary

ASPECTS: The position of the planets in relationship to each other, measured by degrees with the 360° circle of the Zodiac. (See Fig. C)

ASTROLOGY: The science of foretelling events, making predictions, and delineating personality, based on the study of the heavenly bodies. The study of the influence of the stars on the destinies of man.

DECANS: A succession of 36 fixed stars, which rise approximately ten days apart. Also, the division of each sun-sign into three sections of ten days each: the first decan; the second decan; the third decan.

EPHEMERIS: A chart showing the positions of the planets at a given time, used by astrologers in drawing a horoscope.

HOROSCOPE: A chart showing the division of the twelve houses of the heavens, with reference to the position of the planets at any given instant, within the figure of a circle. (See Fig. B)

HOUSES: The twelve divisions of the horoscope, representing a phase of the life of the native. See page 19.

LUMINARIES: The sun and the moon, which are generally loosely referred to as planets.

PLANETS: The heavenly bodies with whose positions astrology is concerned. They are: Mercury; Venus; Mars; Jupiter; Saturn; Uranus; and Neptune. Some astrologers also include Pluto.

QUADRIPLICITIES: Grouping of sun-signs into "families" of four each. They are:

    Cardinal: Aries; Cancer, Libra; Capricorn

    Fixed: Taurus, Leo, Scorpio, Aquarius

    Mutable: Gemini; Virgo; Sagittarius; Pisces

SUN-SIGN: The section of the Zodiac pertaining to the date of birth of the native. Each of these has a mythological name, and a symbol. See page 11.

TRIPLICITIES: Grouping of sun-signs into "families" of three each, representing the four ancient elements of life.

    Fire: Aries; Leo; Sagittarius

    Water: Cancer; Scorpio; Pisces

    Earth: Taurus; Virgo; Capricorn

    Air: Gemini; Libra; Aquarius

ZODIAC: An imaginary belt encircling the heavens, divided into twelve parts, each called a "sign", and each represented by a symbol. (See Fig. A)

I. Introduction:
What the Stars Say

YOU are a unique person. Just as the markings on your fingertips belong only to you, so do your personality, fortunes and destiny. Astrology can help you to lead a happy and successful life. How? By showing you what your individual talents and capacities are, and how you can develop them. "Know thyself," said the sages. This, then, is the purpose of this book: to help you know yourself, and through this self-knowledge, to find the answers to some of life's perplexing questions.

Before we delve into what astrology can do for you, let us find out what astrology is. Its basic tenet is that the pattern of the stars and planets in the sky at the time of birth determines the personality of the native. Based on a chart, called a horoscope, an astrologer can not only delineate the personality of the subject, but also predict how the changing patterns of the skies, in years to come, will affect him.

This much-maligned science is neither witchcraft nor magic. It has been written about by the great poets; it has found its way into every major religion in the world. It has been subscribed to by great scientists, including Copernicus, Erasmus and Newton. Moreover, it is a system that is rooted in antiquity, whose first stirrings predate the written word itself!

"I don't believe in astrology," says the skeptic, unaware of the fact that his own daily life is influenced in every way by it! Our calendars were first planned by the earliest mathematicians,

the Babylonian astrologers. Our wedding ceremony customs, the
honeymoon in particular, are astrological in origin. The twelve-
man jury we think of as belonging to our modern life, was
begun by the Greeks, who felt that a fair trial was guaranteed
by having a representative of every point of view on the jury—
one man from each of the twelve signs of the Zodiac.

Biblical scholars readily admit the influence of astrology in
the Christian religion. The Holy Book itself is full of astrological
references. The twelve tribes of Israel represent Zodiacal signs.
The three wise men were astrologers. "Unto all things there is a
season," says the prophet in Ecclesiastes. "And there shall be
signs in the sun and moon and stars," the Gospel according to
St. Luke tells us. Finally, because Christianity has both Judaic
and Greek roots, we see that it has, of necessity, taken much
from astrology. At the time of the birth of Christianity, astrology
was in full flower in Greece. Its laws were the laws of the land,
and just as it became part of the Greek pagan religion, so did
it flow into the Christian.

"No reasonable person could believe in astrology," the skeptic
argues. No? But Plato did, and in fact outlined in his *Laws* a
composite god, Apollo-Helios, in which the god of mythology
was united with the sun itself. Socrates further based his observations on the nature of the universe upon astrological data. When
the great Sir Isaac Newton was challenged by Sir William Halley,
the astronomer, upon Newton's "superstitious" belief in the
celestial science, Newton replied, "Sir, I have studied the subject.
You have not."

"Astrology is for the ignorant," the skeptic continues. Yet he
can cast no aspersions upon Shakespeare, who wrote: "It is the
stars, the stars above us, Govern our Condition." Shakespeare,
too, put "Beware the ides of March" into our vernacular, as he
told of the astrologer Spurinna's warning to Caesar. Dante was a
believer in astrology; the *Divine Comedy* contains many such
references. "Ye stars which are the poetry of Heaven. . . . In
your bright leaves we would read the fate of men and empires"
Byron wrote. This list could go on and on, for the numbers of
great men of the ages who "followed the stars," is legion.

The story of astrology tells the history of our civilization. It was not only Caesar, Tibernius, and Nero who relied on the advice of astrologers. The British government, during the time of World War II, employed an astrologer, who headed a special section of British Intelligence. His purpose—to predict what Hitler's astrologers were advising the Nazi forces to do—and so to anticipate Hitler's actions!

Ancient art that it is, astrology's uses today are numerous. Dr. C. G. Jung, one of Freud's most important disciples, found horoscopes of his patients to be more reliable in predicting personality traits than such universally used diagnostic methods as the Rorschach test. Astro-medicine was one of the oldest branches of the celestial science, and yet people today are surprised to find that its tenets, which were examined, gathered and tested through the ages, still hold water. Interviews with prison and mental hospital attendants show outbreaks of violence are at a peak during the full moon. Records in maternity wards show a 25% rate of increase in births at the time of the new moon— hardly surprising—astrology has said so for generations!

On and on the story of astrology's achievements goes. It is not the purpose of this book to "make a case" for the influence of the stars. *As in every other area in which man's mind alone must bridge the chasm between that which is based on tangible evidence, and that which must be taken on faith, there are no final proofs.*

It is true that there have been many inaccurate predictions made by astrologers. There have been countless prophets who, using what they believed to be accurate astrological data, have made dire predictions of the world's imminent ending, and other deductions just as far-fetched. Recently, a foremost American pictorial magazine published an article on astrology, in which it was predicted that England's Princess Margaret Rose would not marry until 1961. Many, many astrologers erred in predicting the results of the 1960 American presidential election.

How then, in view of these facts, can astrology be justified? It can be justified in the same way as other theories which are practicable, but not infallible. Voltaire defined medicine as a science in which "The physician prescribes drugs, about which he knows little, for a human body, about which he knows nothing." Surely, appalling errors have been made in the practice of medicine, and yet no rational person would argue that medicine is a hoax!

Perhaps the most reasonable justification of astrology was made by the great naturalist, John Burroughs, who was a friend of astrologer Evangeline Adams. When asked why he gave credence to astrology, he replied that he had found in nature that everything influenced everything else, so why should man not be influenced by the stars? And it is true that the moon's pull over the tides will affect even a teaspoonful of water; that flowers inevitably turn toward the Sun; that geologists have established that earthquakes relate to Uranus' aspects. Why, then, are we to assume that man is less a part of life, less tied to the stars, than the other creatures of the earth and sea?

Astrology represents man's search for the answers to the baffling questions of life and creation. As we have seen, it dates from the very dawn of civilization. Scholars place its birth in Mesopotamia, at least 5,000 years ago. It spread to India in about the 6th century B.C., and then to China. In Greece, astrology became fully developed; in fact it was here that it became the dominant influence on religion, philosophy and science.

Using the Egyptian concept of the horoscope, the Ancient Greeks developed astrology's methods. The Egyptians, in order to tell time by the sky, had selected a succession of 36 stars, which they knew to rise at ten day intervals. These stars are now known by their Latin name: *decans*. These *decans* were grouped, three to each sign, thus forming today's twelve-sign Zodiac. The Greek word, *horoskopos*, from which the word horoscope comes, means a "decan star."

Now, let us see how astrology works. Visualize, as did the founders of astrology, the sky as a great circle, divided into twelve pie-shaped wedges. Each of these represents one of the twelve signs of the Zodiac. The Sun, the most important influence in astrology, occupies one of these sections for about one month each year, moving counter-clockwise. The signs of the Zodiac are:

Aries the Ram (March 22nd to April 20th)
Taurus the Bull (April 21st to May 21st)
Gemini the Twins (May 22nd to June 21st)
Cancer the Crab (June 22nd to July 23rd)
Leo the Lion (July 24th to August 23rd)
Virgo the Virgin (August 24th to September 23rd)
Libra the Scales (September 24th to October 23rd)
Scorpio the Scorpion (October 24th to November 22nd)
Sagittarius the Archer (November 23rd to December 22nd)
Capricorn the Goat (December 23rd to January 20th)
Aquarius the Water-Bearer (January 21st to February 19th)
Pisces the Fish (February 20th to March 21st)

Corresponding to each of the signs, there are distinct types of personalities. Find yourself and your friends and family, in the paragraphs below:

Aries (March 22-April 20) : You are the natural leaders of the Zodiac. Pioneering, courageous, dashing, you enjoy nothing more than a challenge. You are champion of the underdog, and defender of the weak, a person of both ideals and action. You love a cause, the more unpopular the better!

You are quick in your movements, witty in speech. You are always a good companion. It is easy for you to make friends; you like people around you. Romantically you are eager—even ardent. You love adventure, admire achievement, and search out excitement. Life with you may be a headache, but it never is a bore!

Aries is a powerful sign, and whether you are a power to the good or not, depends upon you. Nikita Khrushchev is an Arien. Anyone who has seen the television report of his rage over the workings of a U.N. meeting, will remember the scene during which he pounded his shoe on the desk! Here is Aries' dark side! On the other hand, rational, brilliant, humane Thomas Jefferson, whose concept of government remains America's highest vision, was also a native of Aries!

You sons and daughters of Aries have the ability to take the reins of life into your own hands. You can make your life what you will it to be.

Taurus (April 21-*May* 21) : Tenacious, practical, steady, and reserved, you quietly achieve just what you set out to do. You are an excellent planner, and a reliable, careful worker. Great physical endurance is one of your gifts; you make full use of it. You have excellent self-control, and can discipline others as well as yourself.

There is a second side to your nature. Besides being level-headed and clear-thinking, you are also a lover of beauty. You have fine and luxurious taste. In fact, many natives of this sign are highly talented, particularly in music. You are romantic, but you are inclined only toward deep and lasting love. You have a pleasant and even disposition, unless really goaded, when you display a fierce temper.

Taurus is the sign of the "do-er." For sheer tenacity, and strength of purpose, Taureans have no peers. These qualities are all the more impressive, because they lie behind a deceptively placid and easy-going exterior. Paul Revere, of the famous "Midnight Ride," was a native of this sign. A veritable genius, he was America's foremost silversmith, and a most important artist of his time. But Taurus does not make for an ivory-tower existence! No remote dreamer, he, but the patriot whose courage in the face of disaster is retold in every American history book!

Gemini (May 22-*June* 21) : You are among the most change-able and unpredictable people in the Zodiac. For you, variety is truly the spice of life. If your mode of existence does not provide enough stimulation, you will quickly stir up some excitement. However, you are not the butterfly you may appear to be at first glance. Gemini natives are highly intellectual, with a particular affinity for literature. Words are your natural forte; you speak and write with facility. You are mentally agile, and learn quickly. Versatile, you pick up new skills at once.

Romantically you are flirtatious, and alas! rather fickle. You are a charmer, and make conquests with no difficulty, but it requires real effort for you to settle down to domesticity.

You are somewhat hard to understand, for your personality contains so many seeming contradictions. You reserve the right to change your home, your job—and most of all, your mind—without warning. Geminian Ralph Waldo Emerson summed up your philosophy when he wrote, "A foolish consistency is the hobgoblin of little minds." It is not so much that you mean to baffle, but rather that you so quickly become bored with one way of life.

Cancer (*June 22-July 23*) : For you, "home is where the heart is." Loyal and tenacious in love, you are completely family-centered. It is there that you dare to express yourself, and there that you find comfort, for you are sensitive, easily-wounded, and rather timid. You are however, also generous, sympathetic, and responsive. You would rather give than receive. But this does not mean that you are not shrewd in business. On the contrary, you are thrifty, far-sighted, and can succeed even at great odds. You are honest and reliable. Your approach is usually conventional; you do not like innovation. You are intuitive, and may even tend toward mysticism, but you conceal these traits, for you do not like to be thought "different."

Cancer rules not only the home, in an individual sense, but also the homeland, itself. Patriotism is a Cancerian attribute. Perhaps this accounts for Cancerian song-writer Irving Berlin's authorship of such songs as "God Bless America," and "Over There." George M. Cohan, too, proudly proclaimed his feeling for his country—whose "birthday" he shared, when he wrote: "I'm a Yankee Doodle Dandy. . . . Born on the Fourth of July."

Leo: (*July 24-August 23*) : Leo's symbol is the Lion, and like the "King of the Jungle," the native of this sign must be master

of all he surveys. Napoleon and Julius Ceasar were natives of
this sign. Not all those born under Leo rule empires, of course,
but it is true that natives of no other sign take as naturally to
leadership, as do those of this fifth Zodiacal sign.

You were born not only to command, but to love, as well.
You must be adored, or you are miserable. You are magnanimous
—in fact, "generous to a fault," is a Leo expression. Large-
hearted, kind, you are never guilty of any pettiness or miserliness.
You are just and frank, honest and noble in purpose.

For you, "All the world's a stage." You have a strong sense of
drama, and display it in everything you do. Frequently you are
accused of being theatrical; but this is no affectation. Rather, it
is an important facet of your personality. It will emerge whether
you are actually part of the theatrical profession, or not. The
Leo histrionics were on display whenever Leo Durocher's team
played, for he was a native of this sign.

Virgo (August 24-September 23) : Yours is the gift of intelligence. Shrewdly analytical, logical and observant, you enjoy
nothing more than working a problem through to its conclusion.
You are inventive and ingenious. "If a thing is worth doing, it is
worth doing well," must have been first phrased by a Virgoan.

You respect knowledge, and have wide interests. You have
unusually high standards, which make you critical of anything
or anyone who does not measure up. You work both yourself and
those around you to the point of exhaustion.

You are in constant search of perfection. This is the reason
that so many members of your sign have reached the highest
pinnacles in their chosen fields. Leonard Bernstein, Theodore
Dreiser, Leo Tolstoy, and George Gershwin, are among those
who distinguished this sixth Zodiacal sign.

England's great Queen Elizabeth I, was a native of Virgo. It
was under her sovereignty that England defeated the Spanish
Armada, and became, for the first time, a great empire. But
perhaps, even more important, it was during her reign that
England's art flourished, and such names as Bacon, Raleigh, and
the great Shakespeare himself dominated the world of letters.

Her encouragement, no doubt, was behind England's rennaissance. Virgo, you see, represents not only the practical and down-to-earth aspects of life but the very highest octaves of art and culture, as well.

Libra (September 24-October 23) : A feeling for beauty, harmony and justice rules your life. You are usually surrounded by people, for you have an inborn ability to be tactful and agreeable. Although secretly you may suffer over the unfairness of life, your sweet and generous nature is always on the surface. You are flexible, adaptable, well-balanced. You can influence others gracefully, and rarely lose an argument or make an enemy. Although you are highly creative and responsive to art, your work may not lie in these fields, for you have good business judgment, as well.

No better example of the Libran personality can be cited than President Dwight Eisenhower. Well-known as one of America's most beloved figures, it is said of him that he never made a personal foe in his life. Regardless of political affiliation, everyone who has ever come in contact with him has found him a most likeable, kind person.

Scorpio (October 24-November 22) : You are a creature of extremes. Scorpio is a dual sign, and as its native, you have many sides to your personality. Yours is the strongest sign in the Zodiac. You can be as much a power for destruction as you can for creation. Dominant, shrewd, ruthless, and passionate, you may be loved or hated, but never merely tolerated.

The physical side of your nature is highly developed. You are magnetic to the opposite sex. In this area, as in all others, you usually conquer. Obstacles of any sort mean nothing to you. You are both analytical and intuitive. You have tremendous energy and perseverance. You seek success, and nearly always find it.

You are your own worst enemy. You can be bitterly sarcastic, if you choose. On the other hand, you have a deep and mystical understanding of life, and so possess sympathy and empathy.

Natives of your sign often find brilliant success. Scorpio is the

"President's sign"; more presidents of the United States were born under your star than under any other. Outstanding among them was Theodore Roosevelt, whose affable, jovial exterior concealed a singularity of purpose and strength. A rugged individualist, he was nevertheless able to inspire the love and confidence of the masses. "Speak softly, but carry a big stick," he advised. A good point to remember, Scorpio!

Sagittarius (November 23-December 22) : In a word, you are a "square shooter." Direct, honest, and charming, you are probably the best liked person in your crowd. Because of your manner, you can say and do things that would be bitterly resented coming from anyone else! You want others to be as honest with you as you are with them. Nothing irritates you more than a "phony."

You loathe restrictions, and are happiest when completely independent. You like travel. You enjoy learning, you have good concentration, unless you are interrupted in the middle of a task; then you have difficulty resuming it. You are unusually competent, energetic, active, and achieve much in your busy life.

Winston Churchill possesses the "typical" Sagittarian personality. The "V" for Victory sign that became his trademark, stands for a number of qualities of his own character, as well. Valiant, of course. Verbal, too, for who can forget his "blood, sweat, toil and tears" speech, a priceless piece of oratory that inspired a generation to its deepest level of sacrifice, and its highest peak of glory.

Capricorn (December 23-January 20) : Practical to the core, an accurate and dedicated worker, you are determined to achieve success in your undertakings. Because you are so ambitious, and set such high goals, it may take a long time, but you are patient! You are inclined to be a slow starter, but work willingly toward your ends. You assume responsibility gladly; in fact you have a horror of being dependent on others. The expression "Yankee Trader" suits your personality. You are shrewd, and drive a hard, but fair, bargain.

Capricornians are often accused of being cold and undemonstrative. Actually, you love deeply, but have difficulty expressing your feelings. You believe that your actions speak louder than words, anyway. There is nothing of the flowery romantic about you. You are unpretentious, honest, plain and good as the earth. Those whom you allow to really know you are aware of your fine qualities, your loyalty, reliability and keen sense of obligation.

Albert Schweitzer exemplifies the very finest type of Capricornian. Devoted to his cause, the cause of all humanity, he seeks neither fame nor admiration. Yet, the very calibre of the man has brought to him the appreciation of the entire world.

Aquarius (January 21-February 19): Astrologers seem partial to this sign, calling it the "sign of genius." Surely the list of famous people who were born while the sun was in Aquarius, is impressive. A quick rundown includes such names as: Francis Bacon; Robert Burns; Lord Byron; Lewis Carroll; Mischa Elman; Somerset Maugham; Mozart; Edgar Allen Poe; Charles Dickens; and of course, our great President Abraham Lincoln.

As an Aquarian, you are above petty considerations. You are outgoing, dedicated, giving. You are devoted to all humanity. You are completely honest and truthful, and in fact, worship truth for its own sake.

You have an acute mind. You have a wealth of interests. You are rarely bored, and never boring. You approach every subject with an open mind. You have no personal prejudices, but rather are totally tolerant.

You have a somewhat detached air about you, which is caused by your preoccupation with your original ideas. You belong to a sign which numbers among its members the instigators of change and progress, the developers of all that is humane, just and democratic in our civilization.

Your sense of belonging not only to your own environment, but to all mankind, is evident in your attitudes. It was no accident that Aquarian Franklin D. Roosevelt addressed the

American public as "My Friends"! Yours is the sign of the brotherhood of man. You are truly, "your brothers' keeper," an exponent of the golden rule.

Pisces (February 20*-March* 21) : You may be as mysterious to yourself as you are to others, for yours is a truly mystic personality. You are keenly intuitive—in fact, even psychic. You have a spiritual approach, a sympathetic understanding of people, and a deep empathy for others.

Yours is a dual nature. On the one hand you are honest, hardworking, methodical. On the other, dreamy, moody, impressionable. You are an idealist, and are cruelly hurt when your beliefs are shattered. Seeking harmony, beauty, and peace, you dislike the discovery that life is far from perfect!

Material matters may not be as important to you as the things of the spirit. In fact, you prefer solitude and contemplation to active striving for achievement. You have, most likely, a good deal of artistic feeling and ability. However, your perceptive nature makes you wise in the ways of the world, and so chances are that you have inherent business sense. Success often seeks out natives of your sign.

Pisces is traditionally given domain over the unknown and uncharted. It has sovereignty over the seas, for instance. It is interesting how the precepts of astrology, an ancient science, are applicable to the constantly changing world in which we live. For instance, what could fill the definition of the "unknown and uncharted" better than outer space? Here we see, convincingly, Pisces' influence. Not only did three of the original six astronauts have this sign prominent in their charts, but the first man who ever went into outer space, Yuri Gagarin, is a native of Pisces!

Before we complete this section on the signs, a note must be added. If you were born on one of the first three or last three days of any sign, you are on the "cusp." If you were born, for instance, on March 22nd you must read the sections on both Pisces and Aries. If your birthday is April 21st, you combine the qualities of Aries and Taurus. Such people are more complex than those who have birthdays during the middle of any sign.

You may have noticed, if you read the descriptions of each sign in the preceding paragraphs that there are similarities in several signs. This is not coincidental. Signs form "families."

Aries, Leo and Sagittarius belong to the "fire" trio. Natives of these signs, like the element itself, are volatile, excitable, flamboyant.

Taurus, Virgo and Capricorn, are earth signs. Natives born under these groups are practical, down-to-earth, conservative.

Gemini, Libra and Aquarius are "air signs." This is the realm of thought, ideas, reason.

Cancer, Scorpio and Pisces are "water" signs. Natives of these signs, like the sea itself, are slow-moving, deep, quiet, mysterious.

So much for the signs. They will be referred to continually in this book, for it is the occupation of the Sun in each sign that determines, in the main, the personality of a person.

But let us go back to the "great bowl we call the sky," in order to learn further how an astrologer delineates your character, or predicts what the future holds for you.

Each of the twelve signs we have read about represents not only a Zodiacal type, but also signifies a "house." In general astrology, Aries is the first house, Taurus the second, Gemini the third, Cancer the fourth, and so on. However, in the solar horoscope, the houses are counted beginning with the native's own sign. For instance, if you were born on June 1st, you are a Geminian, and Gemini is your first house. Cancer is your second house, Leo the third, Virgo the fourth, and so on in order around the Zodiac. If you were born on December 1st, you are a Sagittarian, and Sagittarius is your first house, Capricorn your second, Aquarius your third, etc.

Each of the twelve houses represents a separate area of the person's life. Here is a brief description of each:

House 1: *The self, the personality and disposition.*
House 2: *The money and possessions of the individual; ambitions, etc.*

House 3: *Intellectual qualities, self-expression, writing, communication.*

House 4: *Domestic concerns, home, estate, inheritance.*

House 5: *Children, love, pleasure, amusement, theatre.*

House 6: *Health, work, service given to and by the person.*

House 7: *Partnership, marriage, cooperation and joint endeavors.*

House 8: *Death, regeneration, sex.*

House 9: *Philosophy, travel, religion, the higher mind.*

House 10: *Career and status, responsibilities.*

House 11: *Hopes and desires, interest in humanity, friendships.*

House 12: *Limitations, both self-imposed and imposed by others, inhibiting factors.*

Now, these houses have occupants. The sun, as we have noted, moves continually through these signs. In addition to this most important star there are others with whose movement astrology is concerned. They are: the Moon; Mercury; Mars; Venus; Jupiter; Saturn; Uranus; Neptune; and Pluto. Like the Sun, each moves in its own orbit, some quickly like the moon, others slowly, as Neptune through the Zodiac. *At the moment of your birth, a map was formed just as at this moment, another is now in the heavens. It is the pattern formed by these planets that is charted in your horoscope.*

Let us see what qualities the planets themselves have so as to understand what their placement in the horoscope means.

The Sun is the parent of the entire solar system. It is the ruling sign of Leo, and is also particularly important in the charts of those born from April 1st-10th, June 11th-June 21st, the last week of August, November 1st-10th, or January 11th-21st. Well aspected, it makes the native strong, cheerful, masterful, confident. It governs the public life, and its goal is life's highest fulfillment.

The Moon has dominion over the sensitivities, dreams, moods of the individual. It is a feminine planet, and is more important in the chart of a woman than of a man. It rules liquids, the sea, travel and travelers. It is the ruling sign of Cancer, and is important in the charts of those born during the periods of June 22nd-July 23rd, May 1st-10th, September 20th-30th, December 1st-10th, and February 10th-19th.

Mercury is called the "heavenly messenger." It rules communication, speech, writing, all phases of the intellect, and thought. A true son or daughter of Mercury is quick, restless, moody, bright. It is particularly important in the charts of those born between August 24th-September 23rd, May 22nd-June 21st; for it has dominion over the Virgo and Gemini signs. It also is prominent in the charts of those born between April 20th-30th, July 1st-10th, November 20th-30th, and February 1st-10th.

Venus is the Goddess of Love and Beauty. It rules peace, adornment, artistic endeavor, luxury, harmony. She is the Goddess of entertainment, parties, flowers, perfume, play, and in short, the niceties of life. It is the significator of the woman he loves, in a man's chart; and in a woman's chart shows her approach to love. It is dominant in the lives of people born under Taurus, and Libra, and also those during April 11th-20th, the last ten days of June and the first ten of September, November 11th-20th, and January 21st-31st.

Mars is the God of War, and the ruler of the masculine elements, in a personality. It is by nature fierce, fiery, active, energetic. Well aspected it gives great courage, daring, initiative. Its negative aspects are hostility, destructiveness, impatience. It rules a man's sexuality, and in a woman's chart signifies the type of men to whom she is attracted. It rules the sign Aries, and has particular force in the charts of those born in Scorpio. Other Martian decanates are January 1st-10th, March 12th-22nd, and June 1st-10th.

Jupiter is called the "greater fortune," and is the most lucky of all planets. Well aspected it brings success, fortune, glory and happiness. It rules abundance, optimism and judgment. In determining whether a move is favorable or not, an astrologer first notes this planet. Jupiter is the ruler of the sign Sagittarius, and you have a Jupiterian influence in your chart if you were born between November 23rd-December 22nd, in the last ten days of May, the first ten days of August; between October 15th-24th, and December 20th-30th.

Saturn is called the "Celestial Taskmaster." It brings discipline, delay, and ultimately, through tests of character, strength. A poorly-aspected Saturn makes for pessimism, despair and gloom. Well aspected, it makes the native intensely practical and able. It is said that the hardest lessons we learn are the ones Saturn teaches us. It helps us to overcome obstacles, and properly used, brings success. Saturn has dominion over the sign of Capricorn, and you have a Saturnian influence in your chart if you were born between December 23rd-January 20th; May 13th-21st, the last ten days in July or the first ten days of October.

Uranus is the planet of invention. It has dominion over the inventor, and also altruism, originality, progress, aviation, electricity, and ingenuity. It is an erratic and unconventional influence, and more than anything, rules the unexpected. The true Uranian native is a really extraordinary person, and one who truly understands the concepts of universality and brotherhood. It reigns over those born under the sign Aquarius, and is powerful in the charts of those born between January 21st and February 19th.

Neptune is the planet of vision, and of the subterranean and submerged aspects of life. It is mysterious, mystical, romantic and yet remote. Badly aspected it makes for deception, lies, drug and liquor addiction. Well aspected it is enobling and beautifying. Neptune is particularly forceful in the charts of those born between February 20th and March 21st, for it rules Pisces.

These descriptions of the planets are brief, and omit many phases. It further must be noted that the quality of the planet depends to a large measure on the sign in which it is found. For example, Venus in her own sign of Libra is soft and feminine, and makes for a romantic, gentle person while if Venus appears in the native's chart in Aries, it denotes a fickle, careless influence in romantic matters.

One further explanation will complete our very brief description of the workings of astrology. The planets, as they travel around the Zodiac, make "aspects" to each other. They are either in the same sign, at any given date or in a different sign than other planets. The aspects are: conjunction; sextile; square, trine; opposition. Aspects show good tendencies and traits, or adverse ones. Again, these interpretations are subject to modification according to the benificence or malignancy of the planets involved. For instance, Sun trine Jupiter is very fortunate, while Jupiter trine Saturn is somewhat neutral. Saturn square Mars, for instance, is a difficult aspect in a chart.

We have seen how each house, planet, and aspect has dominion over certain areas of your life. In certain positions the planets make you cheerful, capable, fortunate. In others, they impose restrictions. The study of the interpretation of a chart is highly complex, as you can see, for there are so many factors involved in each reading. Perhaps one of the reasons astrology often gets a public "black eye," is that a truly competent astrologer is very hard to find. Most people are too careless to devote the considerable time and study that astrology requires.

If you were to have your horoscope drawn up by a good astrologer, it would be a costly and time-consuming process. But then, of course, you would know a great deal about yourself. Every planet, every aspect, would be properly accounted for, and you would have a chart that would belong only to you. *However, for general purposes of character interpretation, the placement of the Sun, alone, is sufficient. Simply by knowing the date of your birth, you can know many significant facts about yourself.*

Now, what does all this mean to you? Simply this: *as a part of nature, you, as every other living creature, respond to cosmic force. You cannot alter the paths of the stars. You cannot change their influence. What can you do? You can learn to take advantage of the stars. You can plan your life so that you are in harmony with yourself. You can learn to modify your traits, within the framework of your own character. You can learn to understand others, to know with whom you can live and work happily. You can use this wisdom to find the answers to life's major problems.* And surely this can mean the difference between a life that is fruitful and successful, or one that is a failure.

This is the message the stars hold for you!

II. Make the Most
of Your Personality

IF you could be anyone you wanted to be, whom would you choose? Do you envy the life of a certain movie star, for instance? Or would you rather be an historical figure, or a statesman, or even, perhaps, your next-door neighbor? Chances are—after all the choices are reviewed, after the pros and cons are weighed—you will realize that for every gift the gods give us, a penalty is imposed. No one has enough beauty, enough charm, enough wisdom, or even enough luck, to lead a truly charmed life. Life is no kinder to the great beauties of the world than it is to their plainer sisters. The lives of many great men were filled not only with tragedy, but with a day-to-day feeling of despair and inadequacy. After all, the person you are best off being is—yourself!

Of course, there is no way of changing your identity. You cannot, for one minute of your life, trade your being for another's. Even in moments of deepest empathy, each of us retains the qualities of his own person, his or her own uniqueness. All that we can do—and this is a goal that is within the reach of everyone—is to be our best selves.

How can we achieve the perfection of our own characters and personalities? Easily enough, in a three-fold manner:

First, we must understand ourselves, as we are now.

Secondly, we must know what we want to be.

Thirdly, we must apply the power that exists in all of us—

the ability to improve ourselves by developing our assets, and conquering our failings.

Robert Burns' immortal poem contained the lines: *"O wad some pow'r the giftie gie us, to see oursels as others see us!"* Here indeed, is a *pow'r* worth having! How much tragedy could be avoided if we did not have instead, the *pow'r to* delude ourselves! How much better off would we be if our rationalizations did not lead us to call our shortcomings by pretty names: honesty, instead of brusqueness, courage, instead of callousness, and so on.

We are all given clay with which to work—the basic putty of our own personalities which we can mold and form. How do we determine what we want to achieve, to what use we want to put our talents and abilities?

First, of course, we all seek love. We want to be the sort of person who can be lovable. Secondly, we want to feel useful. There is little in life that is as satisfying as the knowledge that we are fulfilling our functions in life. Thirdly, we want to be admired and respected. Then, too, we want the material things that success can bring: comfort, luxury, leisure, beauty.

Astrology can help us with all of these goals. *The study of the heavens teaches us that our stars do not determine our lives. They only cause certain proclivities, certain talents, certain personality traits that are inherent in us.* From then on—it is up to the individual. For instance, Taurus can bestow a character that is reliable and dependable—or one that is stolid and dull. Pisces can incline its natives toward sensitivity—or to morose moodiness.

You can't make a silk purse out of a sow's ear, says the adage. On the other hand, pigskin has its uses, too! There is no one who cannot, by work and concentration, improve himself. Find yourself in the paragraphs below, and learn how you can make the most of your personality.

Aries (March 22-April 20) : You have an impressive personality. There is no one who is less likely to be a "face in the crowd" than an Arien. You are an individualist—unique, strong-willed, forceful. You may be cheered, or jeered at, but one thing is certain—you will never be ignored!

You have an alert and powerful mind. You are quick; you grasp ideas immediately. Conversation with you is always stimulating. You are keenly interested in other people. They, in turn, confide in you readily, not because you are gentle and sympathetic (for actually you have rather a brisk approach), but, rather, because you immediately get the gist of the subject, and have a genuine desire to help. You can be relied upon to give frank advice—sometimes brutally frank, in fact!

You believe that life is in your own hands. You have little patience for waiting anything out. You do not believe much in fate. For you, existence is action. You are in the forefront when it comes to making changes. "Don't just stand there," you say, "do something!" You are among the least helpless members of the Zodiac. Much of your motion may be only "sound and fury, signifying nothing," but move you must, anyway!

In any crisis or emergency, there is nothing like having a quick-acting Arien around. There is little that you fear. If you do happen to be afraid of something, you cannot rest until you conquer it. You are courageous in every respect, and in no way more truly than in casting out the hobgoblins in your own mind.

You are what you seem to be. There is little sublety, and no artifice, in your make-up. People understand you readily. For one thing, you express yourself honestly, openly, and—often! What is on your mind is on your tongue. Even if you wanted to, and you almost never do, you can not deceive anyone who knows you for more than an hour. In a sense, there is something simple, childlike and direct in your nature, and it is immediately evident. People either like you a great deal, or strongly dislike you, and there doesn't seem to be too much you can do about it.

Unfortunately, although you are perfectly clear to your friends, they are mysterious to you! You have no ability to judge people. You miss the nuances of character completely. You measure others quickly by external values. You are not blessed with the gift of insight. That is why you are so frequently disappointed in your relationships. You must, above all, learn to hold off on your decisions, to give some time and thought into measuring character. This is a particular problem in romance. You have a brilliant mind, and a lively intellect, but you don't use it at all in your personal relationships.

You are a totally spontaneous person. Debbie Reynolds is a typical Arien. Her vivacity, her fresh, mischievous mien, are traditionally found in people of this first sign. Marlon Brando, another Arien, demonstrates the qualities of the sign. A rugged individualist, he. Who else but an Arien would have dared to shock Hollywood by riding through town on a motorcycle, a pet chipmunk perched on his shoulder!

You possess many appealing personality traits. For sheer charm, you are way out front. Intelligent, amusing, witty, you are a wonderful companion. Your courage, your strong opinions, your very uniqueness, make you a memorable person.

But on the debit side, you have your share of red marks! For one thing, you are apt to be restless and impatient. You are so forthright that you often leave a wake of hurt feelings behind you. You must learn to think before you speak. Remember, other people may be far more sensitive than you imagine.

Because in so many ways you are naturally superior, you may be arrogant. It may shock you to learn this is one of your faults; chances are you are totally unaware of it. Deep down, you want to be liked. Not everyone can keep up with you, mentally or physically, so have a little more patience with people. Curb that tongue! You don't mean to show off—secretly, you are a simple and humble soul. Make sure you do not give the wrong impression.

Taurus (April 21-May 21): You are the salt of the earth. Dependable, determined, responsible, mature, you are the sort of person whom everyone admires. You are a rock and a fortress, literally a tower of strength to all those who are close to you. You are, too, kind, gentle, loving. You possess an unbeatable combination of personality assets.

The late Gary Cooper personified the traits of your Zodiacal sign. A soft-spoken and gentle man, he possessed a rare blend of sophistication and simplicity. This combination appealed to people of every class. No intellectual, he nevertheless numbered among his close friends such mighty luminaries in the world of ideas, as Ernest Hemingway. He was received and loved in the highest society, without ever losing any of his unaffected candor. Herein lies the charm of a Taurean.

You are fundamentally a practical person. You are not likely to go off "half-cocked" on wild schemes and unusual ideologies. You keep your head and your balance. You appreciate a touch of the exotic in your friends, however, and do not ask that others conform to your ideals. Your ability to accept people just as they are is a definite asset in your romances and friendships.

You have, among your other good qualities, a great deal of self-control. Although you have a strongly sensual streak to your nature, you keep it concealed. You practice self-restraint to such an extent that no one guesses your inner nature is far more passionate than your placid exterior indicates.

Your down-to-earth approach is evident in your sense of pleasure. Anything in which you become interested, must make some appeal to senses. You are not dominated by your intellect; on the contrary, you are a physical creature. You never propel yourself into doing something on the grounds that it will be "good" for you. Either you derive satisfaction from it, or you forego the activity.

You are loyal. Once you have found a friend, you stick to him through thick and thin. In fact, you have a tendency toward blind devotion. But if, on the other hand, you are not attracted to someone, nothing can make you change your mind. No one can be as cold and indifferent as a Taurean, if he so chooses.

You are demanding. You give freely of yourself, and by the same token, you expect this in return. You want the person in whom you are interested to drop everything else at the very sight of you. Unhappily, it does not always work out that way, and then you are bitterly hurt. You become disillusioned by any behavior on the part of others that does not meet your test of loyalty. You want others to return your dogged devotion, your unswerving allegiance.

You have, by and large, an even, pleasant disposition, and an easy-going manner. It takes a great deal to enrage you, but when you finally do get angry, you are just like a bull before whom a red flag has been waved! Woe betide the person who pushes you to this point! Your rages are monumental, and you neither forgive nor forget!

You have many endearing facets to your personality. Calm, natural, warm, magnetic, and charming, you are likely to be loved and respected. Your honesty, your straightforwardness, are much in your favor. Your innate goodness is a virtue.

On the other hand, there is much for you to overcome. And overcome your faults, you can, for you possess determination and will power. Here is the bad news: you may be stubborn, even to the point of being pig-headed. Your over-conservative attitude may be a handicap, for it can prevent you from experiencing many of the exciting adventures in life. Another problem is that you hate to be contradicted. You do not like to take even constructive criticism. Likewise, you do things rather slowly, and become angered if you are hurried.

Your personality has a wonderful potential. Make the best of yourself, and you will find that you gain not only the esteem of others, but an inner feeling of value, as well.

Gemini (*May* 22-*June* 21) : "Do I contradict myself?" asked Walt Whitman, a Geminian. "I contain multitudes." And there is the secret of your personality!

You have a dual personality. On the one hand, you are sunny, charming, witty, gay. On the other, cynical, flippant, moody, irritable. But even on your cloudiest days, you possess a great deal of charm—more so, in fact, than perhaps any other member of the Zodiac.

Primarily, your appeal is that of the intellect. You have an agile mind, and most of your life is spent in learning. You absorb all that comes your way; you are alert and make use of everything you learn. You have an open mind, and so are receptive to new ideas. Life does not easily shock you. You have few preconceived prejudices.

You are versatile. Your friends find you a wonderful companion. There are few occasions on which you do not show up well. You are as happy amid intellectual surroundings as you are on the dance floor or the playing field. You can find fun, pleasure, and new experiences in nearly every endeavor. Life is rarely dull, in your opinion, and this attitude is contagious.

You have a great deal of "get up and go." In fact, change and variety are as important to you as the very air you breathe. You become bored and restless when you are faced with the same dull routine every day. You are a charming and gay companion when you are happy, but you make no attempt to hide your restlessness and short-temper, when you are bored.

This sign rules language. You are an adept conversationalist. You have a gay and sparkling wit. In fact, many outstanding comedians, including Bob Hope, are natives of Gemini. Sometimes, unfortunately, your repartee becomes a bit too crisp, and you strike people as being sarcastic. In fact, there is a certain rather taunting side to your conversation. You are extremely impatient with people who cannot match your agile mind, and then you cannot resist a barb or two.

Basically, you are sophisticated. Simple pleasures, plain people, ordinary experiences, do not appeal to you as much as does the exotic and glamorous. Glamor, itself, is a goal of yours. You like the life of "high society." An interesting facet of your personality, is that you have a unique ability to rise above your beginnings, and to change your outlook, your behavior, even your appearance, almost at will. The career of Geminian Marilyn Monroe, whose climb from an orphan home to the peak of success, demonstrates this quality. It is interesting to note, too, that Miss Monroe displays typical Gemini traits in her dual desire to be both the "sex Queen," and the intellectual. The Duchess of Windsor, too, demonstrates the Geminian ability to advance oneself. Born into a far from wealthy American family, she has made herself into the very personification of international society, and very nearly became the Queen of England!

You are something of an enigma to your friends. In the first place, although you make friends rapidly, you do not form lasting attachments. You do not really give of yourself, in friendship. Critical and analytic, you can find faults in those who are nearest and dearest to you. If you feel that they no longer have anything to offer you, you can cross them out of your life without a second thought.

Although you are the epitome of charm, you have your drawbacks, too. If you are one of the less developed members of your sign, you may be rather superficial emotionally. The weaker type may even be considered cold and heartless. One finds, too, that the Gemini cleverness may be improperly applied—even to the point of becoming slyness—and that the natural mental superiority may result in intellectual snobbery.

Of course, you do not want to have these character flaws, and you can avoid them, by allowing your emotions to show through, rather than constantly subverting your heart to your mind. Remember, that in order to be a truly well-rounded person, you need to let your heart speak, too.

Cancer (*June* 22-*July* 23) : Of all the signs of the Zodiac, Cancer bestows upon its natives the most loving, giving, sympathetic personality. Yours is really the open heart, and the open hand. The expression, "a friend in need is a friend indeed," describes you perfectly.

Although your personality is, again, a loving one, it is not an outgoing one. You save your deeper emotions for those who truly matter to you—your family, your dear friends. You do not make a good first impression, for you hold yourself back, somewhat. You may be inclined to be rather shy and retiring, at first meeting. In any event, you are reserved rather than ebullient and gentle, rather than over-bearing. It takes a long time to know you well, but the end result is certainly worth waiting for!

Like the crab, which symbolizes your sign, you can withdraw into a shell when you are threatened. You have the tenderest feelings possible, and the most innocent remark, made by a well-meaning friend, can wound you to the quick. Then, of course, you retreat. You do not want to talk things out. If you are once critcized, or misunderstood, you feel rejected, and do not want to make any further efforts. In addition to reacting badly to real hurts, you have a tendency to imagine hurts, and to spend a great deal of time wondering what others say or do behind your back.

Underneath it all, you are sympathetic, kind, and warm. People turn to you when they need understanding. You have great powers of empathy—you can "feel your way" into another's problem, literally taking on the grief and worry of a friend as though it were yours rather than his.

There is nothing shallow and superficial about you. You have few affectations. Endowed with the ability to see through disguises and deceit on the part of others, you have no wish to indulge in them yourself. You do not want to be anything other than yourself.

You have great patience. When life does not go your way, you serenely fold your hands and wait—and wait—and wait! Unlike natives of such signs as Aries and Gemini, who strain and protest against life's delays and disappointments, you feel that you accomplish nothing by stirring yourself up. You are a fatalist, and do not believe that you have much control over your life, anyway. Carried to an extreme, this attitude, of course, can be a major fault, for it can lead to laziness, inertia, self-justification. When everything seems stacked against you, consider the possibility that some of your problems may be of your own making. Before you resign yourself to what you feel is fate, be sure that you cannot help yourself in any way.

The Moon rules your sign, and the Moon has dominion over moods. If you are typical of your sign, you find that you feel energetic and optimistic one day, and the next, for no apparent reason, you are deeply plunged in gloom. To some extent, you will probably have to accept these ups and downs as being natural to your disposition. However, try, when you are depressed, to surround yourself with people who can take you out of yourself. You are very receptive to the moods of others.

Although you have a natural reserve, you are popular with others, for they sense the kindness and compassion of your nature. If you can avoid some of the faults that are assigned to your section of the Zodiac—the tenacious possessiveness; the inability to forgive and forget a hurt; the fatalistic attitude that can make you a pawn of your surroundings—you will be able to develop into the admirable person you can be.

Leo (July 24-Aug. 23) : Generous, magnetic, dynamic, vital, you possess an unforgettable personality!

Leo is a regal sign, and as one of its natives, you are blessed with the ability to command. You are a born leader. You are most likely to be the person in your social circle who sets the pace.

You are vivacious, but you have an innate sense of dignity, too. Although you have a gift for fun, and can make others laugh, you do not do it for the sake of playing the fool. People know that underneath your clowning, you demand and get respect.

You are a determined person. Your lively manner is deceptive, for there is nothing easy-going about you. You belong to the fixed sign group. Like your Zodiacal relatives, Taureans, Scorpions, and Aquarius, you are steadfast and tenacious.

On the surface, you appear to be self-assured, but you secretly have doubts about yourself. You are very conscious of your appearance; a Leo woman is miserable if unexpected company finds her in a housedress and curlers. Likewise, you want to be proud of those you love. Although there is room in your big heart for the "lame duck," by and large you are attracted, in romance and friendship, to a person who makes a good appearance.

You are most magnanimous in giving, both materially and emotionally, to those you love. You adore buying presents. You enjoy entertaining. You are a born "check grabber." Your motto is, "The treat's on me!" Of course, like many other things about your grand-scale personality, this can cause problems. You have a tendency to over-extend yourself, and to allow your generosity to cause you to go into the red.

You can be over-bearing, in your well-meaning way. Sometimes you are so anxious to help someone you love, that you foist your own ideas upon him, regardless of what his desires are in the matter. You are not particularly sensitive to the moods of others. Like the other fire-sign natives, you are somewhat wrapped up in yourself, and do not notice the little hints and clues that others give you.

You are frank, sometimes overly so. However, your good nature and sweet smile make it possible for others to take even your most brusque pronouncements in the spirit in which they were intended. You never mean to be malicious, for malice is not a part of your nature, but sometimes you are not as tactful as you should be.

You have, usually, a good disposition. When you do lose your temper, you "blow off," but then you are immediately sorry for it. You are confused when you encounter vituperativeness and cruelty in others, and you do not know how to fight back. There is nothing vengeful about you. If you are really rejected, you are terribly hurt and disillusioned, and do not give the person who wounded you another chance.

In common with natives of the other fire signs, Sagittarius and Aries, you are rather a poor judge of character. You can be led around by the nose through flattery. Anyone who makes an effort to praise you can usually win you. Because of this quality, you must make an extra effort to judge people for what they are, rather than for what they say about you!

To sum up your personality, you are a vibrant person. You are ambitious, authoritative, aggressive. You have two needs: to command and lead, and to love and be loved. Sooner or later you achieve both goals.

On the negative side, you may be arrogant, loud, "pushy." Your pride may become a handicap to you. Furthermore, you may, if things do not turn out the way you want, bully until you get your own way. Another failing to which you may be prone is showing off, and displaying arrogance and snobbery.

Leo natives have much to recommend them. Nearly always, they are popular and sought-after. Like the Sun itself, ruler of your sign, you give off a glow that warms and comforts others.

You are good company, a loyal and devoted friend. No wonder you can go so far in life, simply by making the most of your personality.

Virgo (Aug. 24-Sept. 23) : Your personality is a blend of many seemingly contradictory qualities. You have a highly developed intellect, a strong critical sense, and probably a considerable amount of artistic and literary taste and talent. At the same time, however, you are practical, plain-spoken, down-to-earth.

Yours is not a showy personality. You do not tend to make a strong first impression, for you are basically reserved and self-effacing. You are shy with strangers, and do not really want to expose yourself until you are sure of your audience.

You are likely to have a sparkling but rather caustic wit, and a unique and highly descriptive way of expressing yourself. You never monopolize a conversation, but anyone who is close enough to catch your "asides" during a party, will undoubtedly be very amused. You have the ability to see immediately, with exquisite clarity, what lies beneath the surface in any situation. You are, in short, nobody's fool!

You are highly sensitive. You are aware of everything about you. You do not miss the undertones in anything. You have a great deal of subtlety in your make-up. You are keenly aware of the smallest details. It can never be said of one of your sign that you are "in a fog." Acute, alert, you make use of all your senses.

You are dependable. If you say you will do something, neither heaven nor earth can keep you from it. Your friends know that you are perfectly reliable, and admire you for this rare quality!

You tend to be a perfectionist, and this is one of the reasons that you are sometimes disappointed in people. You are highly critical, and will pounce, like a cat on a mouse, upon your friends' smallest faults. You need to be more easy-going in order to be really happy. Realize that there are few people who can measure up to your exacting standards, and that in being so discriminating, you are missing out on many experiences that can actually enrich your life.

You seek out cultured people. You yourself are highly edu-cated—either by virtue of a good formal education, or through your own studies and observations. Self-improvement is important in your scheme of things. It is not that you want to advance yourself in the eyes of the world, but rather that you want the satisfaction of knowing that you are constantly growing.

You like to be of service to others. You will happily pass along the name of a doctor in whom you have trust, or give advice on the best way to tackle a task. Natives of your sign are often very handy, and like to make things for their friends. At this moment, the writer is working on a beautiful table, which was designed and built, and given as a gift, by a Virgo friend.

Adventures and heroics mean little to you. You are concerned with what is the normal, daily part of your life. You are not attracted to mysticism, to advanced ideologies, to anything that is not tangible. It is the here and now of life that engages your interest. You are concerned only with practical solutions, not with theories. "Will it work?" is your criterion. You are a truly pragmatic soul.

Your personality has many plus values. You are a working member of society, a useful being. You have a clear-thinking honest approach to the realities of life. You are rarely deceived by rationalizations. You are bright, honest, trustworthy.

On the other hand, however, you tend toward over-caution, over-criticalness, and even narrow-mindedness. You may be so much a perfectionist that you split hairs, and so moral that you may strike others as being a prude. Watch for these negative aspects of your character. You, more than many others, have the perception and intelligence to see yourself clearly. Thus you have the ability to change and improve yourself.

Libra (*Sept.* 24-*Oct.* 23) : As a Libran, your personality is so pleasant and amiable, your kind nature so appealing, that you can be described as a truly winning person.

You can literally "charm the birds off the trees." Like the character in Barrie's play, you know that "charm is a kind of a bloom"—and that if you have it, nothing else about you really matters. You have the soft, sweet aura that makes others want to bask in the radiance you give off.

Behind your charm, of course, lies a true consideration and appreciation of other people. More so than the members of any other sign, you can put yourself in the other fellow's place in a difference of opinion. The golden rule is natural to you; you instinctively treat others as you would wish them to treat you.

You are likely to be placed in the position of peacemaker, for your tact can smooth out the rough spots in life. You have a strong sense of justice, of fair play. You are called upon to make judgments that require the wisdom of Solomon—and if anyone can fulfill this role, it is you!

You enjoy a lively social life. You go out of your way to meet people. Without ever forcing yourself upon them, you can quickly become part of your friends' lives. You are the first in your neighborhood to pay a call to a new neighbor. You remember the birthdays of all your acquaintances; you send thoughtful little gifts. You pay hospital calls, you never overlook anyone at Christmas. You are prompt to write thank-you notes. None of the small courtesies of life are ever beneath your notice.

You enjoy a houseful of guests, and encourage a constant stream of visitors to your home. You entertain graciously. Even unexpected company is sure to find a neat and well-arranged house, a good meal, and you, yourself, in a company mood.

You want much out of life. In fact, you may be disappointed because things do not always work out as you desire. You are, in the first place, rather materialistic. Beautiful clothes are important to you. You would love to be on the "best dressed" list. You put care into your selections, always making sure that every article you choose is of fine quality, and becoming to you. You like a pretty home, expensive furniture, elegant accessories. You may be troubled by envy; if your friends have finer possessions than you do, you secretly fret.

Libra natives are interested in culture. Venus-ruled, you love beauty, and may, in fact, be very creative artistically. You need to be able to express your creativity, in order to be a well-rounded person. A need for beauty, for self-expression, are essential facets of your personality. Despite the fact that she dearly loves her family, a Libra woman becomes depressed if she is tied to her home by *"kinder und kuchen."* She needs to get out among people, to seek recreation outside her home, to develop herself independently of her family.

If you do not find the satisfactions of life that you seek, you may lean toward "escapist" tactics—possibly building up a strong fantasy life. Anything sordid depresses you. You explode rebelliously if you are confronted with a long-term problem in your home or your work. When things go your way, though, you have the pleasantest disposition in the world, display an even temper and a sunny smile constantly.

You crave harmony above all else. You have such a dread of friction that you may become weak and compliant, finding it easier to compromise your principles than to fight for what you intrinsically believe in. People may think you shallow and insincere, because in your need to avoid discord you deliberately misrepresent, flatter, deceive. However, the ability to rise above your weaknesses lies within you, and you can cultivate that nobility of purpose and kindness of soul that are the virtues of Libra.

Scorpio (*Oct.* 24-*Nov.* 22): Power and determination are the keynotes of your personality. You are a native of the strongest sign of the Zodiac. You are, in a word, invincible.

You have surely noticed that you never make a neutral impression. People either love you, or hate you. In fact, you prefer that they do anything rather than ignore you! Dominant, forceful, even ruthless at times, you make your mark upon people, and upon life!

The qualities of your nature are a puzzle to many of your companions. They are bewildered by your combination of passion and reason. Most people are ruled either by their heads or their hearts, but your personality is a product of both emotion and intellect.

But even more than being intelligent, you are philosophical. You are concerned with the very mysteries of life and death.

Your sign rules death and regeneration, and you come closer to understanding the final meaning of existence than do natives of any other sign.

A contradiction in your personality is that, although you are capable of a Spartan existence, if need be, you are really a sensual person. You are given to excesses in food, in drink, and most of all, in love. You are tremendously attractive to members of the opposite sex. You, in turn, find it difficult to resist the allure of romance. From childhood, really, you are geared toward the expression of physical passion, and it requires all your will, sometimes, to keep from allowing this need to dominate your life.

You have a hot temper. When angered, you can strike out so that you make wounds that last a lifetime. In general, you like an argument or dispute, for you enjoy winning. You have a certain amount of difficulty in any human relationship, and you become downright restless when things go too smoothly! You enjoy flaunting your superior strength and intelligence.

There is much in your personality that is fine and good. At their best, natives of your sign are among the most admirable members of society, representing, as they do, the very epitome of courage, wisdom, brilliance, and magnetism.

However, because yours is a character of extremes, your failings loom as large as your virtues. The weaker type of Scorpio native can be quite cruel. He can have resentments that assume unrealistic proportions. He is prone to imagined slights, and can suddenly distrust people who have been completely honest with him.

The basic quality of your nature is this: you are a law unto yourself! You are singularly unconcerned about what others think of you. You chart out your plans, choose your occupation, your companions, your partner, irrespective of what public opinion says. For this reason, because you are unhampered in your decisions by the approval of others, you are able to lead a freer, more vital, and more satisfying life than are your less courageous brothers and sisters.

There is little in life that frightens you. You have strong

physical courage, and strong moral courage. You are at your best under adversity; when others crumble, your true character emerges. You are resourceful, and can make the best of whatever circumstances offer. For one thing, you do not believe that life owes you anything. You do not become resentful when trouble appears; instead you plan your tactics and, like a good General, muster your forces for an all-out battle!

You are careful in your associations. You do not "spread yourself thin" by making friends indiscriminately. Partly this is because you have high standards, and partly because you do not want to expose much of yourself to others. You are secretive. When you are told a secret, you will die with it rather than give it away, and your own inner life is never fully revealed to even your closest associates.

Remember, Scorpio, more than any other sign, bestows will power upon its natives. There is nothing, literally nothing, you cannot change about yourself, if you so desire. You will, if you think it over, find that by keeping your eyes on the image of the sort of person you would like to be, you can modify your weak points and advance your positive side.

Sagittarius (*Nov. 23-Dec.* 22) : Your personality is characterized by imagination, practicality, and most of all, independence. You are a veritable ray of sunshine, cheerful, optimistic, good-humored.

If you are typical of your sign, your personality requires little improvement. You have a host of friends and well-wishers. You are liked because you like people, and can accept them just as they are. You have no patience with dishonesty, but aside from this, there is little else against which you discriminate. You can draw your friends from all echelons, for it is the intrinsic worth of a person that appeals to you, not the external qualities.

Your speech is as direct as the arrow that symbolizes your sign. A Sagittarian can say absolutely outrageous things, and can get away with it! Your frankness can be brutal, but because you mean well, no one takes offense. Even after you "tell 'em off," they remain your bosom buddies. On the other hand, you are, deep inside yourself, something of a shrinking violet. Your feelings are easily wounded. Public approbation is important to you. If you feel someone does not like you, you can be very hurt.

You have a great love of life, and for people. Mark Twain, a native of your sign, exemplifies the Sagittarian point of view very well. Although he had a clear vision of the foibles and frailties of human nature, he found his fellow men both lovable and admirable. His humor, too, is typically Sagittarian. It is a kindly, though sharply accurate wit.

You are truthful, and you like truth for its own sake. There is nothing of the four-flusher about you. You present yourself honestly, and want to be taken—or left—just as you are. You do not indulge in daydreams, nor convince yourself that you are more intelligent, more beautiful, or wealthier than you are. You live in a world of reality. Walter Mitty had no trace of Sagittarius about him!

Your sense of justice is one of your outstanding qualities. You have high integrity and good morals. Religion probably plays a large part in your life; if not formal religion, then surely the precepts of religion. You are interested in the formation of a philosophy of life, and you constantly add to your learning. In time, Sagittarians become truly wise and learned people.

You believe in a balanced life. You find time for intellectual endeavors, but you do not ignore the social pleasures. You enjoy the outdoors, but you are at home in society, too. You are an excellent conversationalist. Your speech is salted with wit. It is as pleasant to spend an evening just talking with you, as it is to join you on the rounds of your many activities.

There is something of the gambler in you, and this trait shows itself in your business ventures, your pastimes, and in fact, your very philosophy. You like to take a dare. You will take a chance on nearly anything, provided there is no danger of compromising your sense of honesty. You are a grand sport—a gracious winner and a good loser. "It's all in the game," you smile, and go on again without rancor.

You, as a Sagittarian, are likely to be one of the most popular members of your crowd. However, every sign has its faults as well as its virtues, and yours is no exception. Sometimes your love for the truth may cause you to be rudely frank. Your direct approach may be interpreted as coarseness. Your exuberance may get out of hand, making you overtalkative. Because you are given to enthusiasms, you may lose sight of what you can accomplish, and find you make plans and promises on which you cannot follow through.

The highly-developed Sagittarian is among the best of people —sensible, intelligent, kind and generous. The faults to which you may fall prey can be easily overcome, freeing you to develop your personality to its highest peak.

Capricorn (Dec. 23-Jan. 20): As a native of Capricorn, you are likely to be a "self-made man"—or woman. Your personality is like a piece of metal that has been forged in fire. You are not one of the lucky ones to whom happiness and fulfillment come easily. Your star is Saturn, the "Celestial Taskmaster." Yours is the "school of hard knocks." Your achievement, your very character, are all the more admirable, for they are the result of your triumph over the problems of life.

People admire and respect you, even, perhaps, more than they like you. You possess, in large measure, the important qualities: strength, dignity, honesty, reliability. There is little about you that is flamboyant. You are serious, hard-working, earthy.

Capricornians dislike living alone, but on the other hand, they find it difficult to form attachments. As a native of this sign, you do not trust others easily. They have to prove themselves to you. You would like to be the center of a large circle of friends, but you do not know how to go about it. You have, beneath your confident exterior, secret feelings of inferiority. You would like to be gayer, less serious, more fun to be with, but somehow, you just can't! For you, life is always real and earnest!

You are very conservative. You are desperately afraid of making a fool of yourself, or of doing anything that will lower your reputation. You want to be thought highly of. You are reserved, and rarely bubble with enthusiasm over anything. You keep your emotions to yourself.

You have an acute sense of obligation. You repay every favor. You go out of your way to avoid being "beholden" to anyone. If someone has done something for you, you never forget it, although you do not express your gratitude in a flowery fashion.

Although you do your good deeds quietly, and without fanfare, you nevertheless are a giving person. A person who turns to you in times of trouble, will find you a source of strength and comfort. You are the sort who does not wait to be asked, but quietly takes over, in an emergency. You enjoy being of service. You will never turn your back on anyone who needs you. You are of real aid, for you have a logical, practical mind, and can find a wise solution to the most baffling dilemmas.

Inwardly, your motivations are a desire for success, and for achievement. You have dogged persistence, and eventually realize your goals. You are not interested in any diversion that will sidetrack you from your purpose. You are cut from good gray cloth, simple, unassuming, but truly ambitious.

You appear to be on a more even keel than you actually are. You are subject to moods—long-lasting ones, too, unfortunately. If you feel that you have been treated unfairly, you brood, and go into a depressed state. You have, at best, a rather pessimistic attitude toward life, and although you call it "being practical," it sometimes leads you to unnecessary gloominess. You must learn how to conquer these low periods, for they deter you from the happiness you seek. Try to surround yourself with gaiety and companionship, and you can counteract this trait.

You have many admirable qualities, and can go far in life through your own efforts. However, there are certain traits which you must try to modify. Sometimes your desire to succeed makes you materialistic, to the extent that you under-rate human values. Your severity, both with yourself and with others, may make you appear cold and heartless. Your critical nature may lead you to narrowness and intolerance.

You, more than most other members of the Zodiac, have the desire to be a better person. It is within your power, for you have a real talent for self-discipline.

Aquarius (Jan. 21-Feb. 19) : Astrologers seem partial to your sign, Aquarius, and to it are ascribed qualities of high emotional, social and intellectual prowess. Your personality does not seem to be marred by the ordinary faults that beleaguer members of other signs.

You are, in the true sense of the word, a humanitarian. Your approach to life is rather impersonal—or perhaps, above the personal. You are concerned with mankind as a whole, rather than with your own small group of friends and family. You are interested in the basic values of life, rather than in personal achievement and success. You are dedicated to truth, to the progress of the world, rather than to the fulfillment of selfish needs and desires.

Because your viewpoint is universal, and you have great depth of character, you may puzzle your associates. Your friends and family admire and respect you, but sometimes wonder if they are really close to you. You seem to have less need for direct contact than do other people. You are, in short, basically a "lone wolf," despite your active concern with the world around you.

There is little in your character that is objectionable. You can mingle on all levels, and yet at the same time, retain your intrinsic individuality. Although in your choice of close friends and partners you are discriminating, you can make casual friends among large groups of people. You are tolerant and broadminded, without any of the meanness and pettiness that mar the personalities of your less advanced Zodiacal brothers and sisters.

You have rather a dreamy outlook. You have a tendency to become very involved with your Utopian ideas and schemes. Sometimes, people talking to you have the feeling that you are miles away, mentally. You can also become interested in one activity, to the exclusion of everyone—and everything—about you. This, of course, serves your purposes, but can be rather maddening to your close friends and family.

You are a member of a fixed sign, and like the natives of Taurus, Leo and Scorpio, other fixed signs, you are singular in purpose. In fact, to put it bluntly, you are inclined to be stubborn. You do not want to listen to advice, although you give everyone the courtesy of hearing him out. You want to learn through your own experience. Once you have your heart set on a course of action, all the warning in the world will not deter you.

You are an individualist. Public approbation plays little part in your life. You know what you want, and how to get it, and you do not feel you have to explain yourself. Some natives of this sign carry this trait so far that they are considered rather eccentric, but again, this does not trouble them. You really are your own man—or woman.

Because you are miles ahead of others in your concepts, you may be the object of a certain amount of envy and misunderstanding. Many people resent what they consider your air of superiority, and your unwillingness to be interfered with. However, you generally win them over to your way of thinking.

The major fault of your personality is that you may be the victim of your own daydreams. You may find it easier to spend your time thinking about what is wrong with the world, rather than going to work on your own failings. Some members of your sign lack "horse sense." A closer contact with reality is one of the things you must strive to achieve. Remember that your humane goals can be put into effect only through down-to-earth methods.

Yours is basically a likeable personality. You have neither malice nor pettiness as a fault. You have a kind word for someone—or you do not mention him at all. You seek peace, and have a diplomatic approach. If you fully realize your potential, you are a true exponent of brotherly love, a large-minded, kind-hearted individual who serves as an inspiration to others.

Pisces (Feb. 20-March 21): Yours is the twelfth—and last—sign of the Zodiac. In a sense, you are the summation of all that has come before you. In your nature are blended the qualities of the other signs, matured, and brought into final evolution in Pisces. You are the sea, into which all rivers flow. The mystics speak of an "old soul"—a soul which has gone through many incarnations, retaining the wisdom of all the ages. In your Zodiacal place, this is what you represent.

Yours is not an easy personality to understand, nor to describe. Your character has many subtleties. Conversely, hard as it is for others to understand you, you can clearly see through anyone with whom you come in contact. You are completely perceptive about people. This is why you are so broadminded. You believe in the Indian proverb, "You cannot judge a man until you have walked in his moccasins." You feel a kinship, and a love for all mankind, and are never intolerant.

You possess rare sympathy and understanding. Without being conscious of doing anything other than being yourself, you have much to give. You are the recipient of your friends' deepest secrets. They know they can tell you anything, for you are never shocked by human nature.

Because you give so much of yourself, you are equally demanding. You are terribly hurt by what you call disloyalty, or when others display what you feel is a lack of confidence in you.

The impression you make on others is that you are dreamy, idealistic, sensitive. You are very easily upset by sordid aspects of life. You are deeply sensitive, easily wounded, and perhaps even rather shy and timid. You are very conscious of your own limitations—much more so than you should be. You require from others a great deal of encouragement.

Yours is a spiritual nature. You must have solitude, in order to develop. You do badly in the hustle and bustle of the everyday world, and although you can cope with it for periods of time, eventually you must find some sort of retreat. This does not represent an escape from your responsibilities, but rather an ascension to a higher level, where you can permit your creativity to assert itself.

Many Pisceans are mystics, with a deep interest and understanding of life. There is a touch of the Oriental in your philosophy, for you believe in thought, rather than activity. Zen Buddhism, for example, is Piscean in concept.

You are moody; more so, in fact, than natives of any other

sign, except perhaps Cancer, with whom you have a great deal in common. Sometimes you feel that you are the "goat"—that others step on you. This, of course, is not the fact, for rather than being looked down upon, as you imagine, in your periods of depression, you are much admired for your wise and kind nature.

The hardest lesson you will have to learn, is to conquer your own self-doubts and timidity. You have, when you are hurt, a way of cutting yourself off from others. Do not give in to this tendency. Learn to believe in yourself, and to have faith in the kindness of others, for the world will treat you much more fairly if you do.

III. Pick a Partner

"LOVE makes the world go round," says the adage. Possibly. At any rate, it is the stars that make love go round, it seems. In no other area does astrology have so much to tell us, as it does about romance. Venus herself, the Goddess of Love, reigns over affairs of the heart. The planet of beauty, art, music is also ruler of that mysterious, exciting, and most enjoyable of all occupations—falling in love!

Evangeline Adams, the most famous astrologer of our times, claimed that in almost every instance, the first interest a woman client had was in the placement of Venus in her chart. Well, why not, for as Byron said, "Love is a woman's life entire." And love, to a woman, is composed of so many elements: her ability to attract a partner; the wisdom of her choice; her future as a wife, and finally, as a mother. Small wonder the most important aspect of a woman's chart is the ruler of love!

What do we look for when we pick our partners? The adage tells us that opposites attract. Surely that is true—at least partly, for we do seek in others what we ourselves lack. Psychologists tell us that when we fall in love, we are looking for an idealized image of ourselves. So perhaps the perfect mate is one who supplies the elements we miss, and at the same time, is enough like us to understand us. Not an easy order!

It is interesting to compare, or rather to contrast, the qualities that are sought in partners by members of each of the sexes. Men admit that it is the physical attraction that first catches them, but in looking for a wife, they value qualities of character. The perfect wife, most men agree, is one who has a good disposition, loyalty, intelligence, the ability to make a comfortable home, and to be a good mother.

Women, on the other hand, claim that they are not as much attracted by physical appearances as men think they are. The female of the species is looking for a mate whose character is strong and honest. They place great emphasis upon reliability, mutuality of interests, ability to provide materially for a family, and the qualifications necessary to being a good father. Rhett Butler may be the dream hero, but the desirable husband is a much more prosaic, practical man!

Statistics tell us that we Americans now have the youngest average marital age in our history. Today's brides and grooms begin housekeeping at a much earlier age than did those of a generation or two ago. Whether this is a blessing or a problem is debatable, but it is certainly true that these figures indicate that youngsters are making the most important decisions of their lives at a very early age. Many educators feel that courses in marriage and family living should be part of the high school curriculum. At any rate, this is something that parents should bear in mind in raising their children: young people should receive training and guidance, in order to be able to choose their mates wisely, and to make happy homes of their own.

It is not only teen-agers who encounter problems in the seeking of partners. The fact that our divorce rates are the highest in the world, and that the rate of divorce becomes progressively higher for each subsequent marriage, indicates that the problems connected with love and marriage are not as easily solved as the fairy tales tell us. Many, many of us do not "marry and live happily ever after."

You have undoubtedly noticed that you get along better with certain types of people than you do with others. "He (or she) is (or is not) just my type!" we hear frequently. Why? Well, astrology provides many of the answers. We learn that certain signs are compatible with others; certain signs, in combination with others, lead only to friction. The typical romantic, effervescent, exuberant Leo native, married to a taciturn, thrifty, conservative Capricornian, for example, may anticipate a rough road ahead with many compromises necessary.

Of course, if you were to use the birth-chart in forecasting the probable success or failure of any romantic venture, as do the natives of many Eastern countries, you would have to know a great deal more than just the sign under which the people involved were born. You would have to know all the aspects in a chart that indicate the love life. In a woman's chart, the placement of Venus indicates her romantic nature; in a man's chart, it is Mars. Conversely, the man (or men) she will love is indicated in a woman's chart by Mars, and the girl of his dreams shows up in a man's chart as Venus. The Sun in a woman's chart determines the personality she prefers in a man; in a man's chart it is the Moon. Such indices as the rulership and general aspects of the seventh house (the house of marriage), the fifth house (the house of love and children), and the fourth house (the section of a chart dealing with the home life of the native), are of primary importance. Furthermore, it has been this writer's experience that the squares of Saturn to the Moon have much to do with divorce. Complicated? Perhaps, but not to a student of astrology. However, from the preceding lists, you can see that it is not enough to say simply, for instance, that Taurus and Virgo are mutually harmonious, or that Cancer and Libra are not a good combination.

Now, what can the sun-sign alone tell you? A great deal, indeed. If you are a representative member of your sign, and most of us are to some degree at least, you will have many of the qualities ascribed to it. You will be either romantic or realistic, sunny or morose, gregarious or introverted, as the sign prescribes. By learning what your own tendencies are, as well as those of your fiance, or spouse, you will have some insight into whether or not you can live together in harmony.

It is the purpose of this chapter to outline the general characteristics of each sign, in regard to what each of you seek in a partner, can offer to a mate, and generally set as your goals in love and marriage. *Remember, here, as in every area of your life, you can modify your personality.* Find yourself in the paragraphs that follow, and learn the pathways on which your stars lead you in your search for love and happiness.

Aries (March 22-Apr. 20) : "In the Spring a young man's fancy lightly turns to thoughts of love." And you natives, as the personification of the Spring season, find romance your medium. You are eager for experience, courageous with your emotions. You enjoy adventure—and what is a greater adventure than falling in love!

Aries women typically have a great deal of charm, and are attractive. They are considered good sports and good companions. An Aries girl can laugh off a shower at a picnic, or make a joke when the waiter spills a tray full of food on her best dress. With her high spirits and sense of fun, she is in great demand as a date. Underneath her wholesome exterior lies the heart of a flirt, though, and far from being a platonic friend, she captivates the hearts of her boy friends.

The men of this sign, too, are very attractive. The late Errol Flynn, who had Aries prominent in his chart, typifies the swashbuckling appeal of Aries men.

As an Arien, you are fickle. Just as you fall in love easily, you fall out, too. You tend to have many romances as youngsters, and even in maturity may retain a roving eye. Then, however, you rarely pursue the object of your affections, for once you are committed, you are faithful.

You have certain problems, romantically. You are not by nature a good judge of people, and are easily deceived. You are particularly susceptible to flattery. If you are one of the impulsive Ariens who marry early in life, you may be regretting it bitterly. A native of this sign gains maturity and wisdom only in middle age. The choices you men and women make when you have passed the age of thirty or thirty-five are good, and these provide lasting matches.

Aries women are exciting wives. Remember the song that said: "You may have been a headache, but you never were a bore"? That's an Aries wife, for you! These ambitious women propel their husbands into success. Youthful always, interesting and witty, they are fun to be with. Their partners draw from their very vitality.

On the debit side, the Aries woman is often overly-aggressive. It takes a strong man to keep her in her place—and paradoxically, she is happiest when she is being dominated, provided it is by someone she respects! In her home, she is anything but a tranquil influence, and does not have the ability to create an aura of peace and rest. Furthermore—she is jealous!

Aries husbands are chivalrous. They put their wives on a pedestal. It is rare, indeed, to hear a man who is a native of this sign criticize his wife in public. He may drive her to drink at home, but abroad he has nothing but compliments for her.

An Aries man likes to be looked up to. The woman who can make her man feel like Sir Galahad is guaranteed a happy and faithful husband. She will always have to watch the budget, by the way, for her man is extravagant. It is something of a struggle to domesticate the Aries male. He is not naturally endowed with a strong sense of responsibility, and often takes rather a casual approach toward those who rely on him.

Since you, as an Arien, are a positive person, you need to choose a partner who can handle you with tact. You need someone who can give you the serenity and stability that may be missing from your personality. You need a partner who can retain his own personality, and not surrender completely to your will, for you loathe a "doormat."

Ariens are most compatible with people born under the signs of Taurus, Gemini, Leo, Sagittarius, Aquarius and Pisces. They have difficulty getting along with Cancer, whom they find slow and moody; Libra, whose love of harmony strikes them as indecisive; and Capricorn, whom they find overly conservative and lacking in imagination.

Taurus (Apr. 21-May 21): Being in love is as natural to you as breathing, for the ruler of your sign is Venus, the planet of love. In your youth, you Taureans are likely to have many romances. Warm and affectionate, you are very attractive to the opposite sex. However, it is marriage that interests you, and not a succession of love affairs. It is toward this goal that you work.

The Taurus woman has an easy, pleasant disposition. She loves to be wooed. Here is the girl who can really be won with "bon-bons, poetry and flowers." But underneath it all, she is intensely practical. There is nothing impulsive about her choice of a partner. It reflects careful consideration. And when she marries, it will be for keeps. Conditions have to be nearly unbearable before a Taurus woman will break up a home, particularly one in which there are children.

A Taurus woman knows she has much to offer a man—her good looks, charm and taste, her outstanding domestic abilities, her sweet nature. In return, she demands a lot. She wants a partner who can bolster her security, both emotionally and materialistically. Taurus is fond of the good things of life. It must have been a Taurus woman who originated the saying, "It is as easy to love a rich man as a poor one."

The Taurus husband is an almost ideal mate. He is reliable, faithful, generous, and domestically inclined. He likes to be boss in his own home. The true male of this sign is really a man a woman can lean on!

Members of both sexes of this sign are deeply passionate. The Taurean is not always at ease verbally, so while he may not have the pretty words, his actions speak louder than words. He is truly romantic. These men and women make excellent marriage partners in every sense, and are good parents. In fact, they feel that marriage's prime purpose is to raise a family.

Taureans are deceptive in one respect. Their placid exteriors are frequently found to hide volcanic tempers. The path of true love may not be smooth with a native of this sign, for he is not likely to vent his emotions spontaneously; instead, he stores up anger until he explodes. Taureans need to remember to control this trait; it is disruptive to good human relations. They also need to avoid being jealous and suspicious.

Taureans are compatible with Gemini, Cancer, Pisces, Virgo, love and marriage. *Remember, here, as in every area of your life,* Capricorn and Aries. They have problems in their relationships with natives of Leo, whom they find conceited and ostentatious; Scorpio, whose sublety they take as duplicity; and Aquarius, with whom they have no goals in common.

Gemini (*May 22-June* 21) : Your motto in affairs of the heart is: "The more the merrier." Romance is a game to you, and you are not unduly concerned with the hearts you have broken. Fickle and unpredictable, you long to be in love, but have difficulty arriving at that emotion. You are as critical as you are enthusiastic, and one minute the object of your affections seems to answer all your needs, while the next, you see nothing but faults. However, you blithely go on, hoping that tomorrow will bring you the great love you long for.

You desire to express yourself; your romances give you this opportunity. You may enact many a fantasy in the course of a love affair. Actually, you find it difficult to really commit yourself to any experience. Even while you are most a-flutter, the intellectual side of your nature is questioning the emotional one. You enjoy all the trappings of love, and adore flirting. You are a gay and charming companion; you have no difficulty in making conquests.

Gemini women are desirable, sympathetic, and very feminine. Many of them are outstandingly beautiful. Marilyn Monroe, for example, is a native of this sign. The sex appeal of a Gemini woman is downright irresistible.

Gemini men combine charm and highly developed intellect. And they are able to sweep women off their feet. Of course, much of what these men say must be taken with a grain of salt. Blarney is part of the Gemini man's stock-in-trade. They are not only fond of the chase, they are also happy when they are involved in a love affair. These men remain ever susceptible to other women.

As a marriage partner, the Gemini woman has much to offer. She is highly intelligent, resourceful and inventive. Although she is not a natural homemaker, she responds to beauty, and will make sure that her home is attractive and modern. Her very versatility, though, creates problems: she becomes easily bored with the sameness of keeping house. When ennui sets in, it is accompanied by nervousness, and she may become quite dissatisfied with her lot in life.

The Gemini husband retains his flirtatious nature after marriage, but his romances are likely to be in the realm of fantasy. He does not want to endanger his home ties by becoming involved in any indiscretions. He is an amiable and pleasant husband, but—wives of Gemini men, take note!—he cannot stand nagging, and will leave home if he is under constant pressure.

Gemini is compatible with Cancer, Leo, Libra, Aquarius, Aries and Taurus. These natives have difficulties when they have close ties with natives of Virgo, whom they find fussy and exacting; Sagittarius, whose restlessness intensifies their own; and Pisces, whose pessimism and need for solitude they do not understand.

Cancer (June 22-July 23): For a Cancerian, "falling in love with love" is a constant danger. You find life dull without romance. You are temperamentally suited to having close and intimate relationships. When you find the object of your affections, you lavish him—or her—with affection and devotion. A creature of extremes, you give in completely to your emotions. Yours is the classic case of love-sickness; you can't eat, or sleep, or function at all! Your heart does dives and leaps when you see your beloved! You are morose and lonely when you are away from him! Cupid's arrow finds a most sympathetic resting-place in your bosom!

Although you give the impression of being fickle, and sometimes of being cold and unapproachable, nothing could be further from the truth. You may go for long periods of time without being in love, for it is difficult for you to find a person you feel worthy of your heart. You have extremely high standards. Once you find someone for whom you care, you are not easily discouraged. You will, in your quiet way, pursue your lover, even for years. If you are rejected, you carry a mighty torch—again, even for years.

Cancer women are adaptable, and can adjust to whatever role their husbands select for them. As wives they are faithful and passionate. They are excellent homemakers and cooks. They also make outstanding mothers. In fact, one of their problems is that sometimes, once they have a baby in the house, they tend to put their spouses in second place. It is wise for them to remember that their maternal instincts should be applied toward their husbands, too, for most men need to be babied from time to time!

"The way to a man's heart is through his stomach," goes the saying, and women who are out to capture the heart of a Cancer man should be particularly mindful of it! Cancer men love to be cared for and coddled, and above all, fed! These men are handy in the kitchen themselves, too; many a one of them can rustle up a delicious meal.

The Cancer man is a domestic animal. Although his appearance in the outer world may be of aloofness, at home he is warm, kind, gentle—an exemplary husband. He is not easy to snare, for he is wary, but he is certainly worth the effort.

Many Cancerians, particularly the men, do not marry young, for they are reluctant to leave home. The men, more than the women of this sign, may be tied to Mother's apron strings for long after their friends have established independent homes. However, if you are in love with a man born under these stars, you can win him, if you persuade him that he will be as comfortable in his own home as he was in his parents'!

One note of caution must be sounded. As a Cancerian, your emotions run high, and you need to guard against possessiveness and jealousy. "Togetherness" has its virtues, but try to allow your mate some privacy, too. Trust him. You will find that this goes a long way toward smoothing out the rocky road to romance.

Cancerians get along well with natives of Leo, Virgo, Scorpio, Pisces, Taurus, and Gemini. They encounter difficulties with natives of Libra, whose emotions they find shallow; Capricorn, whom they find unromantic and pedestrian; and Aries, whose brusque, plain speech often offends them.

Leo (July 24-Aug. 23) : For Leo, love is all! Like Ingrid Bergman, a native of this sign, you sometimes love not wisely, but too well! Although you like public approbation and approval, you can be made to act so rashly through the force of your own emotions, that you become censured.

However, under the proper circumstances, love has much to offer a Leo native, and vice versa. Leo rules the fifth house, which is the house of romantic love. Without love, you are likely to pine away. You need to be cared for, adored, and even worshipped!

The Leo woman is very attractive to the opposite sex. She has vivacity, charm, and sex appeal. Ethel Barrymore, a native of this sign, set the men of two continents back on their heels, in her day, and today's roster of lovely Leos include such eye-catchers as Lucille Ball, Arlene Dahl and Rhonda Fleming.

The Leo man is an ideal lover. He is passionate, exciting, masterful. He spares no expense when he is wooing a girl; he takes her to the best restaurants and most expensive nightclubs. He sends flowers, cards, and even love letters. He smothers a girl's objections in a shower of affection and attention. In short, he is mighty hard to resist!

Leo natives are sentimental. The young girls are likely to keep scrapbooks full of pictures, dance programs and theatre ticket stubs. They preserve gardens full of pressed flowers, and carefully put away love letters, and other trappings of romance. As adults, they make occasions of birthdays and anniversaries. The women enjoy setting a table for two with candles and flowers, and the men are likely to bring unexpected little gifts for their wives.

The Leo wife is a gem. She is loyal, responsive, completely wrapped up in her man. She is a capable homemaker, and keeps up her own appearance, as well. The husband of one of these women is never met at the door by a frump in a housedress and curlers! She demands attention, and must be appreciated. Unfortunately, she may sulk if she is not given the response she desires. She is a perfect mate for an ambitious man; no wife can provide as impressive a background as one who was born under this royal sign.

A Leo husband is goodhearted and magnanimous. Provided that his family revolves around him, (for he demands this), he is a contented and faithful husband. He wants, and gets, respect at home, which he repays by being a fount of generosity. He is terribly jealous. His wife must be aware of the force of the Leo temper when it is aroused, and remember not to tease him by flirting with other men.

In a partner, you require a foil for your fiery, magnanimous, extroverted nature. You must have someone who can understand that your "Lion's roar" has more sound than fury. You need a mate who can balance your enthusiasms with calm reason, and help you solve the everyday problems of life, which you can blow up to terrifying proportions. On the other hand, you must be careful not to tie up with an introvert, for you love crowds and activity. You enjoy a very social life. You can rarely be happy with a companion who wants to sit home by the fire. The ideal mate for you is someone who is willing to give in a great deal to your wishes. You are a forceful and dominant person, and usually must have your own way.

Leo is compatible with Virgo, Libra, Sagittarius, Aries, Gemini, and Cancer. You will find the natives of Scorpio cold and calculating. In your relationships with natives of Aquarius, you are apt to be frustrated by their impersonal response to you. You find natives of Taurus stubborn and unsympathetic. However, again it must be reiterated that there are many influences in a chart other than the sun sign, and that the person whom you may choose for a mate may not be at all representative of the sign under which he or she was born.

Virgo (Aug. 24-Sept. 23) : An aloof lady, as chaste as the Virgin that signifies the sign, is the classical astrological description of the Virgo woman. But it is this writer's opinion that Virgo is one of the less-understood signs of the Zodiac. It is, for one thing, a dual sign, and like the natives of Pisces and Gemini, other dual signs, Virgoans have two sides to their natures.

In ascribing a cold, cold heart to Virgo natives, astrologers are overlooking the duality of the sign. Many natives of this sign are susceptible not only to romance, but perhaps even to illicit romances. They are flirtatious, in their own way. Many women of this sign are competitive with other women, and are capable of making careful plans to steal the heart of a friend's beau! Virgoans appear to be shy and retiring, but sometimes this cool exterior is very deceiving!

The more common example of a Virgo native is explained by Greta Garbo's statement, "I vant to be alone." One of the most beautiful women in the world, she could have had her pick of the most exciting and eligible men. However, she chose, instead, to pursue a solitary life.

Virgo natives often enjoy flirtation for the sake of verbal fencing. They are keenly articulate, and witty. But underneath the light banter, they are coolly analytic. They weigh and measure the object of their affections carefully. In fact, in this way they sometimes miss out, for romance does not lend itself to painstaking scrutiny. The rough fingers of reality can tear apart the veil of romance itself, and make any affair of the heart commonplace and disappointing.

One of the major problems that confronts you, as a Virgoan, is that you have a fear of being fully understood. You are sensitive. You do not want to risk being criticized, for you expect others to be as critical as you are. You must learn that in order to be happy and fulfilled in love, you must give of yourself without restraint.

The Virgo woman is an excellent wife. She is a top-notch housekeeper, doing her chores quickly and efficiently, and without fanfare. She is a good companion, for she has an active, questing mind, and is usually alert and well-informed.

The Virgo husband is reliable, conventional, a steady provider. Although he may be fussy about health and cleanliness, by and large he is good-spirited and pleasant to be with. He is, by nature, perhaps less interested in the physical side of marriage than are natives of such signs as Scorpio and Pisces, for instance, but he is a considerate and gentle companion.

As a native of this sign, you need a partner who will not demand constant proof of affection, nor bursts of romantic fancy. It is not in your nature to behave in this manner. Furthermore, you must find a mate whose character you respect; you find it difficult to overlook flaws in those you care for. A friendly and outgoing person, whose sunny disposition will act as a foil for your somewhat gloomy moods, is a good choice.

Virgo natives are generally happy with natives of Libra, Scorpio, Capricorn, Taurus, Cancer and Leo. They have personality conflicts with natives of Sagittarius, whom they find irresponsible; Gemini, who strike them as restless and unreliable; and Pisces, whose tendency toward moodiness depresses them.

Libra (Sept. 24-Oct. 23) : A famous story is told about Libran Helen Hayes, the actress who is called the First Lady of the American Theatre. Charles MacArthur, whom she later married, was so impressed with her at their first meeting at a party, that he murmured, as he passed her a bowl of peanuts, "I wish they were emeralds!" The charm and loveliness of a Libran can indeed inspire love at first sight!

As a Libran, you are expert at love. You are affectionate, generous, romantic. You are likely to have many romances, for you are happiest when your emotions are charged. You are likely to have many sudden infatuations, that set you reeling for the moment, and then are just as quickly forgotten. A Libra woman, in giving a friend advice on how to stop carrying a torch, said, "If you are like me, you'll chase one love affair with the next."

You are sentimental. You like to preserve the souvenirs of your affairs. The Libra man is likely to send his love "one perfect rose." Libra women are feminine; many of them give the appearance of being clinging vines. They want their men to put them on pedestals.

Behind the many romances you have, is the constant quest for the right marriage partner, for Libra is the sign that rules marriage. Natives of this sign tend to marry early in life, and have stable, happy homes. The Libra wife creates a harmonious and happy home, and is a fine mother. The Libra husband is passionate and gifted in the art of making love. He requires great affection from his partner, and if he does not find it, may seek greener pastures elsewhere.

As a Libran, there is little about the solitary life that is pleasant to you. You enjoy sharing your interests—music, art and the other finer things of life with some interested audience. You want to maintain all your relationships on a basis of perfection. You are apt to be unnecessarily fussy about the trappings of love, for instance. There is a story that illustrates this point: a Libran woman had planned a lovely dinner à deux for herself and her husband. The dinner was cooked to perfection, the flowers arranged, the candles lighted—and the dinner hour came and went! Fretting and fussing about her husband's lateness, she upbraided him harshly at the door, when he finally did arrive. Perplexed, he listened to her rampage, and then asked, "But is the dinner for me, or am I for the dinner?" The moral is—remember it is the human relations that count, and not the surrounding conditions!

It is not hard for a Libran to conquer the heart he has set out to win. His natural charm insures this. It is somewhat harder, however, for him to live peacefully with a partner, for he has many, many needs that must be satisfied, if he is to find the happiness that is his birthright. He requires love, attention, peace and serenity. He must choose a partner who can, to a certain extent, insulate him from the shabby realities of life. He needs one who enjoys gaiety, humor and romance. A tall order, indeed!

Libra is compatible with Scorpio, Sagittarius, Aquarius, Gemini, Leo and Virgo. You may find friction in your dealings with natives of Capricorn, whom you find earthy and unrefined; or Aries, who are too bold and brash for you. However, bear in mind that most people are a blend of signs, and that modifications are found in each type.

Scorpio (Oct. 24-Nov. 22): Scorpio is the sign that rules physical love. Need we say more!

Scorpio natives are passionate, dynamic, and intense in love. They have a magnetic charm, and rarely lack for attention from the opposite sex. Grace Kelly illustrates the beauty of many Scorpio women, and Burt Lancaster, the craggy-faced actor, typifies the exciting Scorpio man, whom women find irresistible. Yet, you will notice, for all the attractiveness both these people possess, both are happily married and devoted parents. Natives of this sign, once settled, are loyal and faithful.

A Scorpio young man we know, in joking about his love-life, confessed that his first conquest was his kindergarten teacher, who found him so appealing that she kept his little chair next to her desk! Small wonder he grew up with the idea, which was certainly substantiated later in life, that he was very appealing to women!

As a Scorpio native, you are not given to light flirtation. Each romance consumes your whole heart and soul. You have an infallible instinct about people. You know subconsciously who is being honest and steadfast, and who is trying to deceive you. You rarely make any mistakes in selecting partners.

You are a fixed and determined person, and under the excitement of a romance, there is always the search for a mate. Once you have decided on your choice, you will carefully plan the wooing and winning. Again your perception comes into use. You know just what the other person is seeking in you, and how to go about persuading him—or her—that you are the perfect spouse.

Once married, you are happy. However, should you find disappointment in marriage, you become a hellion to live with. You become revengeful, and are heartless in your attitude. "Hell hath no fury like a woman scorned" describes the attitude of a Scorpio native perfectly!

As a Scorpio native, you have a clear idea of your role in marriage. The men of this sign have a deep and genuine affection for their families, but they can be stubborn and selfish. The women, too, if they are catered to, and feel they get enough affection, praise and wooing, are devoted spouses. If not, they can keep the family in an uproar with their temperament and tantrums.

If you have given your heart to a Scorpio native, it is wise for you to bear several facts in mind. First, they do not like to share all their thoughts. They have a strong need for secrecy, and if questioned, will "clam up." Secondly, they tend to be jealous and possessive. Never carry on a flirtation in front of a Scorpio native. He cannot forgive you for disloyalty.

Scorpio is compatible with Sagittarius, Capricorn, Pisces, Cancer, Virgo and Libra. You are bewildered by the impersonable attitude of Aquarians; in conflict with the strong-willed Taureans; and think Leo natives are ostentatious and affected.

Sagittarius (Nov. 23-Dec. 22): "I like a girl who is a real companion; a girl who loves sports and the outdoors, and is always ready to travel, even on short notice," a young man wrote, in a recent magazine article describing the qualities bachelors desire in their prospective wives. The answer to this man's prayers is a woman who is born under the sign of Sagittarius!

If you are a true Sagittarian type, romantic love means less to you than it does to some of your Zodiacal brothers and sisters. Sagittarius is called the "bachelor sign," and it is certainly true that these natives seem less inclined to spend a lifetime in quest of romance than do natives of such signs as Leo or Libra, for instance.

However, as a Sagittarian, you are undoubtably well-liked by members of both sexes. You are sought after for your high spirits and good nature, your easy-going attitude, your humor. A Sagittarian lass is rarely a wallflower.

In romance, you are daring and impulsive. You enjoy dating, and even though you are reluctant to settle down, you have many offers. Your ideals are high, and in order to fully commit your heart, you must truly respect the object of your affections. You are direct and forthright in pursuit of love. There is nothing secretive or underhanded in your nature. A love affair in which you engage must be above-board. You, yourself, are entirely trustworthy, and tend to believe the best about others. Jealousy and possessiveness are rarely faults of the natives of Sagittarius.

In common with the natives of the other fire signs, Aries and Leo, you are prone to disappointments in love, for intelligent as you are, when your emotions are affected, you become rash and hasty. However, you are less likely than natives of those two signs to make an unhappy marriage. When the chips are down, you are careful in choosing your partner.

As a wife, a Sagittarian woman may be a breezy and casual lover, but she is a fine comrade. She fills her home with many friends, and is an excellent hostess. She dislikes the tedium of housework, as she does any job that ties her down, but is efficient enough to complete her chores quickly, and go about doing the things she enjoys. She is happiest when she has personal freedom. For this reason, she must take care not to marry a man who will make her account to him, or who will be jealous.

Sagittarian men have much to offer, but they require very careful handling. In the first place, they are not by nature domestically inclined. These are the men who spend days away on hunting and fishing trips, and put in overtime hours at the office. Community-minded and outgoing, they are active in many fields. The wife of such a man must be the sort who can share his interests, as well as be able to allow him his freedom.

By the way, an oddity of the Sagittarian native, is that although he, himself, is outspoken, and sometimes frank to the point of raw tactlessness, he is very sensitive to the harsh words of others. He cannot bear criticism. Beware answering back a Sagittarian in the same brusque tone he may use with you; it may wound him deeply.

As a native of Sagittarius, you are compatible with people whose suns are in Capricorn, Aquarius, Aries, Leo, Libra and Scorpio. You find natives of Pisces too moody; Gemini natives seem flighty and shallow to you; and you are uncomfortable with Virgoans, whom you find fussy and rigid.

Capricorn (Dec. 23-Jan. 20): Capricorn natives are late bloomers. You are mature as youngsters, but retain the aura of youth until later in life. Beautiful Marlene Dietrich, a Capricornian, illustrates the way in which a native of this sign can remain the object of love and admiration until he or she is a grandparent!

Practical in everything you do, you are no less so in matters of the heart. It is rare for a Capricornian to make an unsuitable match, or marry beneath himself. Although you may have many romances, you do not fall in love easily. You are highly critical. "She thinks she's too good for her boy friends" the mother of a Capricornian miss complained. However, it is this selectiveness that leads to a good choice, and makes for the firm family life a native of this sign needs. Marry they do, and well, too. A Capricornian needs companionship; he hates to live alone.

The women of this sign are not easily led astray by glamor. It is hard to turn their heads with flattery. They want steady and dependable husbands, who will appreciate their competent homemaking.

Men of this sign are good providers, and can be relied upon. However, they tend to be rather autocratic in their home relationships. "Wherever he sits, *there* is the head of the table," said Emerson, speaking, no doubt, of a Capricornian friend.

As a Capricornian, you find the path to romance is often rocky. One of the reasons is that you expect a great deal of others. Of course, you have high standards for yourself, too, but you must remember, in the words of the adage, "no one is perfect."

Another problem that may plague you, is that you have difficulty expressing your feelings. "I told you I loved you when I married you," grumbled the Capricornian husband, when reproached for being sparing with sweet words during the many years of their marriage. He felt, evidently, that the words never needed repeating! Learn to share your thoughts, rather than keep them to yourself. Learn to give others the pleasure of praise and appreciation. Many Capricorn husbands feel that because they support their families, they are showing love, while the women of the sign feel that in cooking for and cleaning for their husbands, they are fulfilling their marital duty.

You are not a "flashy" person. Your qualities of strength of character, honesty, genuine goodness are admirable, but you have a tendency to hide your light under the bushel basket. Get out and mingle with people, learn to be a gayer companion. This will pay off for you romantically.

You have a strong need for security. A Capricorn woman is happiest with a mate who not only provides well for her, but agrees with her theory that it is necessary to save for a rainy day. If she is married to an improvident, extravagant man, she is very tense and worried about the future, and cannot enjoy the present comforts of her life. Likewise, Capricorn men get along best when married to other thrifty souls. A wife who is a free spender can make them miserable.

If the object of your affections is a man or a woman born under this sign, remember that these people are highly conventional. They do not appreciate the bizarre. Avoid wearing extreme clothes, do not indulge in raucous laughter, or tell shady stories, or do anything at all that will make you the object of attention in a crowd. By all means—do not show an interest in anyone else in the crowd! Capricorn backs away from competition.

As a Capricornian, you are congenial with natives of Aquarius, Pisces, Taurus, Virgo, Scorpio and Sagittarius. You do not feel comfortable with the unpredictable, outspoken Ariens; nor with Cancer natives, who tend to bring out the moody and pessimistic side of your nature; nor with Librans, whose manner seems false and affected to you.

Aquarius (Jan. 21-Feb. 19): The expression, "All the world loves a lover" may be turned about to describe the outlook of an Aquarian. Truly, natives of this sign do love all the world, for they are humanitarian and idealistic, and sometimes seem more interested in the world at large than they do in their own romances.

As an Aquarian, you are loyal and constant. You are not given to a number of love affairs. The person who marries a childhood sweetheart is likely to have this sign prominent in his chart. Once your heart is captured, you lose all interest in anyone else. You are unlikely to philander—or even to daydream much about love affairs.

You are attractive to members of the opposite sex, for your qualities of kindness and sympathy. You are an excellent companion—a good conversationalist, who also is a good listener. You are genuinely interested in people, and it is apparent to them. Although you can make friends on all levels, you are not impulsive when it comes to choosing a partner. You set high standards. You seek intellectual abilities as well-developed as your own.

A woman who is out to snare the heart of an Aquarian must remember that he does not like a helpless, clinging vine. He wants a woman he can genuinely respect. Likewise, if wooing an Aquarian girl, remember that she cannot be won with flattery or gifts. She does not succumb to surface attractions; it is a man of character for whom she is searching.

Although you can express yourselves beautifully on any variety of subjects, the words of love do not come easily to you. Particularly if you are married to natives of Leo, Libra, Cancer or Pisces, remember that romance in marriage thrives on small gestures and sweet words!

You are not the sort of person who will concentrate on one thing to the exclusion of everything else. You are likely to have a many-faceted life. Your hobbies, for example, are very important to you. Even when you are in love, you do not devote all your energies toward the object of your affections. You expect him—or her—to understand that you will not be a dedicated and single-purposed lover. You want your loved one to be able to share your interests with you—or if that is not possible, at least you want it made clear that you need free time in order to pursue your other activities.

Life with one of you Aquarians as a mate can be very pleasant. You are reasonable, pleasant, controlled. You do not have attacks of jealousy—or at least, you keep them to yourselves! You do not make unreasonable demands, nor expect perfection. You are always able to compromise, to see the other person's point of view.

It is necessary for you to feel appreciated, but you do not

demand constant proof. You can live happily with a partner whose actions demonstrate that he or she has faith and trust in you. You need a certain amount of privacy, and are uncomfortable when you are in the presence of someone who demands all your attention. Married to a possessive person, you feel hemmed in. On the other hand, of course, you do not want to be taken for granted. It is sometimes difficult for your partner to find the happy medium!

Aquarians are compatible with Pisceans, Ariens, Geminians, Librans, Sagittarians, and Capricornians. Less harmonious signs are Taurus, whose natives you find lacking in imagination; Leo, whose natives demand a greater show of affection than you give; and natives of Scorpio, whose jealousy and possessiveness you find constricting.

Pisces (Feb. 20-March 21):

> *"How do I love thee? Let me count the ways.*
> *I love thee to the depth and breadth and height*
> *My soul can reach. . . .*
> *And, if God choose,*
> *I shall but love thee better after death."*

So wrote Elizabeth Barrett Browning, to Robert Browning, her husband, in one of the great romances in English history. A helpless invalid, she so inspired the love of the handsome and romantic poet, that he literally carried her off, in fairy-tale fashion!

The story of this romance is a truly Piscean one, for Elizabeth Barrett Browning, a native of this twelfth-sign, typifies the sensitive and romantic qualities of the sign.

As a Piscean, you were born for love. You are both affectionate and passionate, and practice the art of lovemaking on both a physical and spiritual level. Your demand to be loved will equal fervor, and require much in the way of catering to and coddling. Your feelings are easily hurt, and one thoughtless word from your lover can quell your fires.

Natives of this sign, particularly the women, are given to

mooning and dreaming about love. You spend a great deal of time in a world of fantasy, and sometimes this is so satisfying to you that you do not make the effort to make your dreams a reality. Men of this sign are likely to have a fear of being hurt, and so are rather timid. They must remember that "faint heart never won fair lady," and be prepared to do something more active about their feelings.

Piscean women are often quite beautiful, in a dreamy way. They can make good use of the soulful eyes and wistful air that belongs to this sign. Lovely Elizabeth Taylor illustrates the charm that these women have for men.

A woman of this sign can capture many a heart, for she is warm and sympathetic, and has the ability to make her men feel loved and understood. These gals are highly sought after, and often make early marriages.

The men of this sign are good husbands. In their romantic manner, they can make marriage a life-long honeymoon. They cherish and adore their wives, and make no secret of it. They want their wives to remain "the sweet girl I married," and enjoy bringing them gifts, flowers, and in general, treating them as though they were still courting them.

The Pisces wife is devoted and faithful. She is considerate of her husband, and puts his wishes before her own. She is thoughtful of his comfort. She has the ability to make her home an oasis of peace for him.

In setting her cap for a Piscean man, a girl must remember that in this case, flattery will get her everywhere! She must make this man feel needed and wanted. As a wife, she may sometimes have to act as a buffer between him and the world, for he is fundamentally a gentle soul, who is easily wounded by the harsh realities of life.

Pisces is compatible with: Aries, Taurus, Cancer, Scorpio, Capricorn, Aquarius. You find natives of Gemini too restless; Virgoans strike you as being over-neat and fussy; Sagittarians do not fulfill your romantic visions, for they are inclined to be too casual.

IV. How to Help
Your Husband Succeed

"BEHIND every successful man there is a woman," we are told. Winston Churchill, whose enviable career has brought him the respect and admiration of people all over the world, is one of the first to admit that he owes much of his success to his lovely wife, Clementine. Former President Harry Truman always refers to his wife, Bess, as "the boss," and in spite of the fact that his friends know he is jesting, he has always felt that his spouse was at least partly responsible for his having reached such heights.

The Victorian lady may have been the power behind the throne, but her gentle voice was never heard voicing opinions about her husband's work. Business was considered a man's domain, and at least by outward appearances, she took a back seat. Today, however, it is a well-known fact that modern marriages are partnerships in every sense. Decisions that concern the family, including ones relating to the husband's career, are made cooperatively.

In the larger businesses, the so-called "organization wife" is a definite factor in her husband's climb up the ladder to success. A research group at the Laboratory of Psychological Studies, Stevens Institute of Technology, found that large firms plan to give wives of would-be executives psychological tests before promoting the husbands. The attitudes of the wives seem to be of great importance in the success or failure of the men.

The last presidential campaign (1960) was certainly an indication of the importance of the little woman. Both Pat Nixon and Jacqueline Kennedy were very much in the forefront, and many a newspaper headline was devoted to the relative merits of each as a first lady. Probably many votes were cast on the basis of whether the honor should go to the patrician, intellectual Mrs. Kennedy, or practical, competent Mrs. Nixon. In fact, even the battle of the wardrobes and hairdos of each was said to have had an effect on the election of the president!

Not only in large companies is the wife important. A small businessman told us recently, "The only reason I could start this venture is that my wife was willing to live on a shoestring until the business got going." In innumerable ways, the attitude of a wife can influence her husband's career. Is the wife thrifty or extravagant? Self-indulgent, or self-sacrificing? Is she willing to travel and able to adjust to new situations, or is she dependent upon the security of familiar neighborhoods and old friends? All these factors must be taken into account.

In their book, *Big Business Leaders in America,* authors W. Lloyd Warner and James C. Abegglen found that the wives of the 8,000 successful executives they studied fell into two major types. One was the woman whose interests lie only in the home, and the other the sort who likes to socialize with company wives and be active in community affairs. Each type was instrumental in her husband's success. The element they had in common was that each felt she reached her highest level of achievement by watching her husband get to the top, rather than by concentrating on her own interests and goals.

Every wife has qualities that sustain and aid her husband, both in his home life and his professional life. Some are at their best actively participating in their husbands' financial affairs, acting as bookkeepers, secretaries, or nurses in their husband's businesses or offices. Others are most effective as hostesses, and can help by entertaining their men's business associates. The woman who can have the boss to dinner and provide a delightful meal and pleasant atmosphere may find that he is more receptive to giving her husband a raise! Other wives find they are better off completely in the background, making their homes a place where their husbands can relax and gain new strength.

The following paragraphs may give you some insight into your own particular abilities. Whether you are an outspoken Arien, or a retiring Cancerian wife, you can be a helpmate.

Aries (March 22-Apr. 20): In the areas of enthusiasm, imagination and ambition, the Aries wife has no peer. She is intensely proud of her husband, and her feelings are not kept secret. She is truly his "number-one booster!" With this faith as a spur, what man could fail?

You first-sign natives enjoy the challenge of a new job, or a job that is too difficult for the average person. You will encourage your men to seek new fields, and conquer them. Defeat is a word that is not in your vocabulary.

As the wife of a businessman, an Aries wife is an asset. You encourage your husband to take the bold risks that lead to the pinnacle of success. A natural optimist, you envision nothing but gain in any venture with which you are connected, no matter how far-fetched it may seem to your more cautious sisters.

You are interested in financial matters—more so than most women—and will lend an interested ear to your husband's shop talk. Although you have no patience for details, you have a swift comprehension of the overall pattern of commerce, and can offer good suggestions. Should problems arise, your brisk approach helps to overcome them. You like to know what is going on, and as you meet setbacks with courage and good sense, your husband can always confide in you.

The Aries' woman's drawback is that she sometimes tends to be so overconfident that she becomes foolhardy. Her impatience needs to be tamed, for nothing worthwhile is built in a day. She needs to learn that the race is not always to the swift. Furthermore, she has to remember that a man's home is his refuge, as well as his castle; she must learn to make efforts to provide a soothing atmosphere. Overcoming these difficulties, she stands as an ideal helpmate for the man fortunate to have her behind him.

Taurus (Apr. 21-*May* 21): Taurus women are particularly cognizant of money and the good things it will buy. They, more than most of their Zodiacal sisters, are anxious for their men to succeed. These women may suffer from feelings of inferiority, and believe that others judge them by what they own. Therefore, a Taurean woman is likely to be very interested in seeing that her man provides well for her and for her family.

Taurus women are very practical. They do not like fly-by-night schemes, and look askance at the idea of quick fortunes. Rather, they will encourage their husbands to work methodically toward a goal, and will see that their men don't lose heart when the going is hard. These natives have fine business judgment, and can give shrewd and intelligent advice. Taurus is the sign of bankers; many a husband of a Taurean woman is glad to have her manage the books in his business.

If you are a true daughter of Venus, chances are your husband is well dressed. If "clothes make the man," as the saying goes, your husband is certainly in luck. You have a good eye for beauty and color harmonies, and can help your man select handsome clothes. You will see to it, also, that he is always neat and clean. Making a proper appearance is very important to you.

Taurus women choose their friends among the rich and affluent. They enjoy all the trappings of luxury and success. For this reason, a Taurus wife can often help her husband make influential friends, who will be an aid to him in his career.

The home of a Taurean woman is pleasant, well furnished, and comfortable in every respect. It is designed for the pleasure of her family. Furthermore, she will cater to her husband—see to it that he has a comfortable chair and good dinner when he comes home at night. Her husband can replenish his energies in his home.

The Taurus woman's main drawback is that she may be stubborn and hard to reason with. If she is married to a man whose ideas are very progressive, she may have difficulty making an adjustment. A further problem is that sometimes her materialism may get out of hand. It is important for her to remember that in starting out in a venture, one usually has to tighten one's belt. If she can triumph over these tendencies, she can be an aid and comfort to her husband in his career.

Gemini (May 22-June 21): Gemini women have the ability to be "all things to all people," and this quality is evident in their relationships to their husbands, too. They can adjust to any role that is required of them. It is the Gemini woman who was probably the first to encourage her husband to take to the new frontiers of this country years ago. These gals love change and challenge. A job transfer is a new adventure; a new business is a great thrill. These women are good partners for men in the armed forces, diplomatic circles, foreign correspondents, and other fields in which travel is indicated.

The Gemini woman is a good hostess. She is witty, charming, always fun to be with. She has the ability to make strangers feel like old friends. In this way she is an asset to her husband in his work, for she can cultivate the friendship of his co-workers and superiors.

The husband of a Gemini woman is fortunate in that he can talk his problems over with her. Although she may not have much "head for business," she is willing to listen. She is reasonable, and open-minded. She does not nag, nor does she harbor grudges. She will not remind her husband of past errors or opportunities lost.

You, as a third-sign native, are a thinker. Although the impression you may make is that of a flighty woman, you are genuinely interested not only in your husband's success, but above that, in his happiness. You will encourage him to enter a field in which he can find gratification, and ignore the fact that his take-home pay may not be high. You understand the real values and objectives in life.

Patience is a virtue you need to cultivate, for you are quick to abandon any project that does not pan out immediately. Remember that there is much tedium in life. Success does not always come quickly, and not all goals can be realized. Most of the time, you are optimistic, but you have your bleak moods, too. Try to keep on an even keel—it will aid you not only in making your marriage happy, but your husband a success, as well.

Cancer (June 22-July 23): Lucky is the man who has a Cancerian wife waiting for him at home. In the warm and loving atmosphere she creates, he can retire each night from his business cares and woes, and emerge refreshed the next morning. These home-centered women are exceptionally talented at creating a soothing base of operations. Being the natural mothers of the Zodiac, they are adept at mothering their husbands.

Because you are a water-sign native, you are intuitive. "I can tell just what went on at my husband's office the minute he opens the front door," a Cancer woman told us recently. "If his footsteps are light and brisk, I tell him about *my* day. If not, I just give him dinner, and settle down to hear about *his* troubles." A perfect example of Cancerian thinking!

The Cancer woman prefers to stay in the background. Even if her husband is in public life, she will not make an appearance unless it is really necessary. First lady Jacqueline Kennedy, a native of Cancer, explains this point of view when she reiterates her feeling that a wife's first duty is to make a comfortable and happy home for her husband and family.

Your homemaking abilities can help your husband in his career, if you wish, for you are an excellent hostess and cook. Many a man has been boosted up the ladder of success after his Cancer wife has had the boss to dinner!

Loyal and steadfast, you brook no criticism of your family. By your loving support, you make your man feel head of his household, and on top of the world! Your only fault as a wife is that you are tenacious, in fact, overly so. Try to avoid the unpleasant nagging you sometimes indulge in. Remember, you can be a great help to your husband if you let him know how much you really believe in him.

Leo (July 24-Aug. 23): A Leo woman will not take a second-best role, nor will these natives allow those they love to be relegated to the background. As a Leo woman you enjoy splendor, luxury, and want to be looked up to and envied. You enjoy being the wife of the corporation president; you can handle this position with *noblesse oblige*. There is nothing petty or mean in you; success does not "turn your head," for you accept it as your just due. You never gloat over those less fortunate than you.

Leo natives enjoy putting up a good front. The young wife of a lawyer we knew felt that at all costs her husband had to have a good address and an impressive office. In her Leonine way, she knew that "success brings success," and was willing to cut corners secretly in order to give the illusion of affluence.

As a native of this sign, you are a hard and tireless worker, and will push yourself to the brink of endurance. You understand the need for hard work, and do not reproach your husband when he puts in long hours at his job, away from you. However, you want him, in turn, to take you into his confidence, and keep you abreast of his progress. You don't want him to indulge in shop talk at parties, to the exclusion of paying court to you. You can best appreciate his efforts to succeed, if he makes you an active part of his success.

In a position in which appearance is important, a man with a Leo wife is favored. Provided you can avoid a natural tendency to dominate—for you need to be reminded that your husband's ego as well as your own, needs nurturing—you are a perfect mate for a man on his way up!

Virgo (Aug. 24-Sept. 23): You Virgo wives prefer to stay out of the limelight, for you are naturally rather shy and retiring. If you are typical of your sign, you prefer that your husband find his career in some field that does not require you to make an appearance. A Virgo wife we knew whose husband was a rising young army officer stationed overseas, complained that, although she knew her husband enjoyed it, she could not help being sorry about his choice of career. She found the very active social life at the base a great trial. She confessed that she enjoyed the variety of the change of locations his work entailed, but moaned, "If I could only avoid those officers' parties!"

Virgo women are happiest when their husbands are involved in intellectual pursuits. A scientist, lawyer, teacher or doctor makes a good mate. Such a man, married to a Virgoan, will find that he has an excellent sounding board at home. His wife will not only be vitally interested in his work, but may even be able to offer advice, too.

Heroics and adventure do not appeal to these women. They distrust anything flamboyant. A Virgo woman, unlike her Leo sister, for instance, cares little for appearances. She is willing to sacrifice in order to give her husband a start. Furthermore, if his work is such that she can be an active partner, so much the better. She would love to serve as secretary, or in a retail business, as saleswoman and bookkeeper. She is content to live simply and to turn the profits of the venture back into the business.

As a Virgo wife, you take good care of your husband. You watch his diet carefully, and see to it that he pays attention to the condition of his health. Your home is comfortable, and beautifully run. Rarely does the husband of a Virgoan woman return to a messy house and a list of tasks she has saved for him to do. He is able to conserve his energies for his work, knowing that the home is smoothly run.

You are paragons, in many respects, but there are pitfalls you must avoid. Because you have a sharp tongue, you must be careful not to undermine your husband's confidence in himself, with unthinkingly harsh criticism. Furthermore, you must know that all success entails risks. Though security is what you require, you must learn to take chances, as well.

Libra (Sept. 24-Oct. 23): How you love success, for money brings the luxury you adore, the beautiful things that are so important to you! You enjoy all its trappings—the gracious home, the pretty clothes, and most of all, the freedom from squalid conditions that you find so unbearable. For these reasons, you Libra natives tend to marry men whom you believe will be able to provide well for you, and will do all in your power to see to it that they live up to their potentials.

There is nothing solitary in your nature. Yours is the sign

that rules marriage and partnership endeavors, and you, as a native, will be sure to have a marriage that is truly a joint affair. You feel that you want to participate in every phase of your husband's work, just as you want him to understand your interests and activities. Because your nature lends so easily to teamwork, you are always ready to entertain in your husband's behalf, and to follow his lead in making new friends, or changing locations. You are fearful that if you present obstacles in his way, through your own lack of cooperation, he may at a later time hold you responsible. You are constantly aware that you want to be an aid, and not a millstone.

Libra natives are highly intellectual and analytical. You can be of real aid in making suggestions regarding your husband's work, for you can quickly understand the existing problems. Even when your emotions are involved, you are able to take a more or less dispassionate view of any situation, and can give good advice.

Of all your many gifts as a wife, your outstanding one is tact. Natives of no other sign can present their ideas so amiably. Although, at times, yours is an iron hand, it is always softly sheathed in the velvet glove. When you feel your husband is off on the wrong track, you are able to influence him so smoothly that he thinks the change was his idea to begin with! Your intense femininity hides the keen edge of your sharp mind, which is surely an invaluable asset to a woman! You are most unlikely to make your husband feel incompetent, or insignificant —even when you both know he has made a whopping error. Instead, in your charming and gentle manner, you create an aura of peace and contentment at home, and so boost your man's confidence in his dealings abroad.

Scorpio (Oct. 24-Nov. 22): Mamie Eisenhower, a Scorpio native, is an excellent example of the way in which a Scorpio wife can help her husband succeed. Although those closest to her know that she is a strong personality in her own right, she has never let any of her desires interfere with her husband's climb to top position in the Army, and ultimately to the Presidency. She herself remarked that their retirement home is their first

permanent home in the forty years of their marriage! For a
woman who is such an exacting housekeeper, the constant moving and succession of rented houses must have been an ordeal.
Yet she gladly put up with all inconveniences in order to help
her husband in his rise up the ladder of success.

As a Scorpio woman, you are unswervingly loyal and devoted.
Although you may scrap privately, you will defend those you
love with all your power. You cannot bear to see your husband
maligned, nor taken advantage of in any way. His happiness
comes first to you. You are a natural fighter, and will perservere
until you get just what you want. In short, you are a power to
be reckoned with!

The pioneer woman, braving the hardships of a new frontier,
signifies the Scorpio personality. Your husband knows that he
is free to make a move for the benefit of his career, even though
it may temporarily undermine the security of the home. You can
take it in your stride unflinchingly. You have great courage,
and never more so than under adversity. This quality of yours
will serve as an inspiration to your man.

Furthermore, you have almost mystic powers of perception.
You can "see through" people, and sense any kind of deception
quickly. You know who can be trusted, and who must be
watched. A Scorpio wife, with her ability to understand people,
can be an asset to a husband in a position that involves any sort
of politics—"office politics," particularly.

Scorpio natives are lucky where money is concerned. They
enjoy owning things. You would rather your husband work for
himself, even if it means a smaller income, than work for someone else. However, there is a paradox in your nature, for while
you can be self-sacrificing, you also can go overboard in spending.
Make sure there is always some backlog in the bank. This will
give your husband the sense of security the head of a household
needs, in order to have faith in his ability to provide for his
family.

Sagittarius (Nov. 23-Dec. 22): As a Sagittarius woman, you like
change, adventure, and have a vast appreciation for the simple,

natural things in life. A life dedicated only to the acquisition of money and possessions does not appeal to you. You will never encourage your husband to plug endlessly in a job he does not enjoy, in order to provide material things for you and your family. Instead, you want him to find personal fulfillment. That, to you, is success.

You have the ability to turn every endeavor into an adventure. A Sagittarius woman, the wife of a mining engineer who was sent to a remote village in Chile, spoke of the experience with great relish. The real hardships of the life were exciting challenges to her. While another woman might have packed and returned to the safety of civilization, she met every day with eager interest. Not all Sagittarians are so adventurous, of course, but as a group you are anything but clinging violets!

As a homemaker, you do not throw the burdens of caring for the house on your husband. You carry your responsibilities and duties through without fanfare. Although the details of housekeeping bore you, you like beauty and cleanliness, and keep a comfortable, restful home. You are probably an excellent hostess; everyone who enters your house feels welcome. You make the home an inviting, pleasant place in which your husband can not only relax, but bring home his business associates, as well.

The husbands of Sagittarian women tend to confide in their wives about their business affairs. These women are understanding, and have keen business sense. They encourage their men to take chances. They believe in expansion and promotion, and are not afraid to take a gamble. Although they may secretly worry, they nevertheless prefer the promise of lucky gains to dull security.

You, as a Sagittarian, must be free to call your soul your own. You will go along with your husband on any venture, so long as you do not feel that either of you are inescapably tied down. A real companion and a good partner, you make a fine wife for a man who is out to find self-expression in life.

Capricorn (Dec. 23-Jan. 20): "Nose to the grindstone" is a Capricorn expression. You are fully aware that success is usually the result of hard, unstinting and self-sacrificing labor. You never berate your husband for not making money quickly, or not rising to the top overnight. You have no patience with laziness or daydreaming, and will work hard alongside your husband, to make your goals a reality.

You want to be respected. You are not the sort of wife who can stay in the background. You know your own worth, and want to be noticed. In a sense you are a snob; you have no patience with people who do not meet your high standards. You would prefer to see your husband in a position of authority, than one, no matter how lucrative, in which his endeavors are unnoticed. In fact, a fault of women of this sign is that in their determination to have their husbands be successful, they may resort to nagging and other pressure tactics.

Ambition is a keynote to your personality. As a career woman you are outstanding, giving your employer his dollar's worth in every way. As a wife, you are just as dedicated. Not only do you like success, but you like work for its own sake. You believe that your husband's truest expression lies in his career. Even in later years, you will discourage your husband if he is thinking of early retirement. You believe there is nothing as rewarding as the attainment of a goal, and the achievement of material success.

Capricorn women are systematic, excellent housekeepers. Your home is not as informal a place as that of your Sagittarian sister, for instance, but rarely does the husband of a Capricorn woman feel uncomfortable at home. He is certainly never going to run out of clean socks or shirts, or find he has to make a hurried trip to the delicatessen to get dinner! You are also very good at managing money, and can make funds go a long way. Chances are that you have taken over the financial side of running your home. Your thrift and shrewdness make you useful in managing business funds, too. If your husband is in business, he well may utilize you as bookkeeper.

One note of caution must be sounded. Because work is your natural forte, and you have great energy and strength for it, do not assume that your husband is also so equipped. Be careful not to push him beyond his strength. Although it is satisfying to achieve wealth and recognition, the intangible things of life are important, too.

Aquarius (Jan. 21-Feb. 19): Money is not by any means your primary interest. Although an occassional Aquarian wife is extravagant, and likes the luxuries of life, by and large members of this sign do not place undo importance either on the acquisition of funds, or on material things. You would rather be looked up to as a contributing member of society, and a force for the betterment of humanity, than as a person of wealth. You do not want your husband to be the most successful man in the community, necessarily, but you would like him to be known as a respected leader of worthwhile causes, and a man of high ideals. You abhor anything that does not uphold both the letter and the spirit of the law. You are repelled by shoddy deals of any kind, and would rather live in simple circumstances than see your husband compromise with his conscience.

"Man does not live by bread alone," is your belief. Your home is one in which there are many activities and projects going. You encourage your husband to find creative hobbies, for you enjoy sharing them with him. You believe deeply in education, and will encourage your husband to take courses and study in order to improve his position.

An Aquarian woman is ideally suited to be the wife of a man who holds a public office, or is in some type of work in which his wife's social abilities play a part. These women like to join organizations, and can do much good for charity.

A real virtue of the wife born under this sign is that she is the least suspicious type in the Zodiac. Although she can be roused to jealousy, being human, after all, she rarely doubts her husband's word, nor does she check up on him when he is gone from the house. A traveling salesman is one type of husband who is well off with an Aquarian wife.

Pisces (Feb. 20-March 21): "She relies on my judgment for everything," the husband of a Piscean woman said proudly. "I enjoy having her call for my help, because it makes me feel important!" Therein lies one of the charms of a Piscean wife. She does not try to overshadow her husband, nor to dominate, but is content to be protected, cared for. She appreciates his strong shoulder fully. This, of course, adds to his self-confidence, and gives him the feeling he can "lick the world." What a boost toward success this can be!

The home of a Piscean wife sometimes has an "other-world" air. It is truly a haven, removed from the worry and bustle of his outside life. Never cold and forbidding, your home encourages your man to be able to rest and relax. You are the sort of person who enjoys dreaming in front of a cozy fire on a cold night, or reclining on a hammock under the trees on a balmy day. These are the facilities you provide for your man.

People are drawn to natives of this sign. Although there is a weaker Piscean type, whose moodiness and self-pity prevent her from realizing her true potential, many of them are among the truly good people of the world. As a Piscean native, you are tops in sympathy and understanding. Your husband knows that you will stand by him, and believe in him through any adversity, never blaming him for his career troubles. You want him to be happy, above all, in his work, and will never place your own interests before his. You can easily adjust yourself to any conditions. You are at your best at providing the spiritual and emotional responses that make your husband a happy and secure person, well able to meet the demands of his job.

V. You and Your Children

"THE hand that rocks the cradle," says the adage, "rules the world." Well, that may or may not be true, but no one can deny that parenthood is an awesome and important thing. Every parent knows that the raising of a family requires every mental and physical effort one can make.

Psychology teaches us that the child is the product of two factors: heredity (the qualities he inherits from his forebears), and environment (the effect of his home, his family and his times). Astrology introduces a third concept, and one that can explain the often tremendous differences that exist between children in the same family. *This is the birth chart, or horoscope of the child, and with it, the knowledge that each person's individual stamp is upon him the moment he enters this world.*

The wise mother knows that she can mold and teach her child to a certain extent, but even as a tiny baby, he has his own likes and dislikes, his own will. Children must be led, never forced, and each child must be helped to utilize his individual abilities and talents. Not by being a carbon copy of his parents, nor the fulfillment of all their frustrated dreams, but only by being himself, can a child grow into a contented and useful adult.

For these reasons, it is necessary for parents to learn not only what their own gifts and shortcomings as fathers and mothers are, but also to have insight into their children. By knowing how you are best equipped to raise your family, and by knowing what you can expect from each child, you can be helped greatly in that most difficult and most rewarding task—being a parent!

The remainder of this chapter is divided into two parts: first, an analysis of you as a parent, and second, your child.

You as a Parent

Aries (March 22-Apr. 20): You are likely to have a large family, for you truly enjoy parenthood. You have a strong feeling of pride in your children. Also, as a native of the sign that rules all youth, you have the ability to reach a child on his own level, to play with him and be a true companion. You are amused and entertained by your children's gaiety and spontaneity, and they find you as original and imaginative as they are. An Aries parent can win the heart of any child.

On the other side of the coin, however, you are apt to be a strict disciplinarian. Aries mothers, particularly, have firm views, and are prepared to back their rules. Although you can make their household chores into games, and even inject your contagious spirit of fun into their attitudes about school, when the chips are down, you want to be obeyed. Furthermore, you have short patience with dawdling, and can never be convinced that all children are natural dilly-dallyers. Moving with the speed of summer lightning yourself, you expect the same of your children!

With all these virtues, it is hard to see how an Arien can fail as a parent. However, there are pitfalls, too. You need to control your temper, for children require great patience, and patience is an unlikely virtue for an Arien! Count to ten before you lose control: your tempers have the ferocity of storms, and can frighten little ones.

Furthermore, as an Arien, you feel a strong desire to be first in everything. You must be careful not to become competitive with your children. You must also remember that their purpose in life is not to shed glory on you. Allow them to make their own mistakes and learn their own lessons. They will not always be a credit to you, but in the long run you will have the satisfaction of knowing that you have done your very best with your children.

Taurus (Apr. 21-May 21): The home of a Taurean is a comfortable and happy place, particularly if there is a little cuddly baby there! Taurus is a most affectionate sign, and as parents, Taureans are warm, demonstrative, sympathetic. Fathers born under this sign are very interested in their children, for they have a feeling for the solidity of family life. It is important, they believe, to have a child carry on the family name.

As a parent, you set high standards for your children. You are orderly, honest, sincere, reliable, and insist that your children learn these virtues at an early age. You like to see your children have the material things they want, but insist that they appreciate and care for their belongings. You do not tolerate anything shoddy or sleazy, and want your children to respect quality.

Taurean parents are patient. Because they are deliberate, and make slow judgments and considerations, they do not rush their children. "Do it slowly, but do it correctly," you insist. You will take the time to inculcate this in your children, and you don't lose heart when you fail to see immediate results.

You must remember that along with your innate talents for parenthood, considerable as they are, are certain drawbacks. It is easy for a Taurean to slip into the habit of being stubborn and unreasonable. You need to tolerate change, for in raising children there is no *status quo.* Their very growth brings about constant change. You do not like to have your routine interrupted. A Taurean woman can become very upset when she has to postpone a task because she is needed urgently by her children.

One further warning: beware of making your children overmaterialistic. Remember that a child is happiest with simple playthings, and with projects, however clumsy, he himself initiates. Don't shower your adolescent with luxury items; give materials which will help him grow and develop, such as musical instruments, athletic equipment, etc., instead of expensive clothes.

Gemini (May 22-June 21): Parenthood is not the easiest state for you natives of Gemini. Although you love your children, and can enter into games with them, you frequently feel tied down and restricted by them. You do not like being in one place long, and children surely do not make one mobile!

The children of Geminian parents are generally early talkers, and usually enter school with a wealth of pre-acquired information. This is because you third-sign parents are highly intellectual and versatile, and love to talk. You confide in your children, treat them as equals, which can make for very close relationships. Occasionally you wonder why your children don't accord you the respect that your friends seem to be shown by their youngsters. The reason is that you prefer an informal, casual relationship, and seldom set yourself up as the stern parent. President Kennedy, a Geminian native, was interrupted at an important press conference by the appearance of his three-year old daughter, dressed in her bathrobe and Mommy's shoes. How typical of the relationship of a Geminian and his offspring!

It is in the area of discipline that you find most trouble. You are lively and affectionate as a parent, but alas, it is hard for you to be firm! You are not naturally consistent yourself, and so lean to inconsistency in dealing with your offspring. Behavior that is criticized by you today will be tolerated tomorrow. Then, worrier that you are, you wonder whether you are failing! Try to remember that children need a certain amount of routine, however odious it is to you. You must never, caught in the flight of your own fancy, make promises you cannot keep. Taking care to avoid these hazards, you Geminians can make delightful, companionable parents.

Cancer (June 22-July 23): Cancer is the sign that rules motherhood. Of all your Zodiacal brothers and sisters, you Cancerians are doubtless the finest parents. You are patient, reliable, giving. You truly adore your offspring. For a Cancer woman, the highest calling is being a mother, and Cancer men are the idols of their devoted children.

True Cancerians have infinite patience with their offspring.

At best, they are sympathetic and genuinely interested in a child's smallest problem. It is this mother who spends endless hours entertaining a sick child, or planning a birthday party that is a perfect delight. Cancer fathers are highly protective, particularly of their daughters.

The difficulties which you may encounter as a parent are seldom evident when your children are small. It is their adolescence that throws you. You enjoy your offspring's dependence upon you, and hate to give up full control. It is hard for your children to convince you that they do not need your constant watchful eye. You are inclined to moodiness and worry, too. How a Cancer father can pace the floor when his teen-age daughter is a half-hour late coming home from a dance!

A further danger that you, as a parent, will have to watch for, is making the children too much a part of your life. Remember that your spouse has rights to your love and attention, too. And be willing, when the time comes, to cut the silver cord, for your goal, after all, is to raise your children to be happy, independent adults. Remember, you can look forward some day to having little ones around again—your grandchildren!

Leo (July 24-Aug. 23): Cornelia, the mother of the Gracchi, must have been a Leo native. It was she, who, when asked why she did not wear jewelry, replied by putting an arm around each of her sons. "Here," she said proudly, "are my jewels!"

Leo rules both love and children. As a Leo native, you love your children wholly and completely. In fact, you frequently fail to see any faults in them. When you do, however, you take immediate steps to discipline them. You particularly dislike lack of respect. You open your whole heart to your youngsters, but it must be understood that they appreciate your efforts. You cannot bear to be taken for granted.

Care must be taken by a Leo parent not to assert too much authority. You are inclined to be a strict disciplinarian, though your children may discover that often your bark is worse than your bite. You are rather stubborn. Learn to listen to both sides of an argument. Learn to be more flexible. Take each day as it comes, for in this, as in other areas of your life, "Life is hard, by the yard; by the inch, it's a cinch."

Sometimes you worry, as do all parents, about your methods of dealing with your children, for you are not as self-confident as you appear. However, you should be comforted by the knowledge that your children are likely to grow up to be secure adults, who will be capable of giving as much love as you have given to them in their formative years.

Virgo (Aug. 24-Sept. 23): Conscientious in everything you do, you do not take the responsibilities and duties of parenthood lightly. In fact, if anything, you tend to worry over small problems that would not trouble others. You take great pains to establish proper habits in your children, in regard to work and diet, particularly. You Virgoan mothers are always sure that your children's meals contain all of the "basic seven." You give a good deal of emphasis to cleanliness, too.

Virgo parents like to see their children established in a routine. Even the most permissive of you insist that your children understand that work comes before play, and that chores must be organized systematically. You insist on homework being done well, and on time. Furthermore, when you give a task, you give letter-perfect directions, and will not tolerate anything half-done.

Virgo fathers are generally not affectionate. Although they love their children deeply, they do not have as much patience, perhaps, as they should. Because they are inclined to be fussy and meticulous, children's haphazard ways and noisiness can be very irritating to them. Virgo mothers have to be sure that they do not allow their own schedules, their super-efficient housekeeping, to become more important than their children.

The typical Virgoan places a great deal of emphasis on matters of the intellect. It is important to you that your children are successful in school. You will make great sacrifices to insure that they go to college, take music lessons, and so on. You are willing to help them, too, with their learning.

Virgo parents have a lot to offer their offspring. They can transmit their own high standards. The children of Virgo mothers are tidy, organized and efficient. Since Virgo fathers are handy, they teach their children useful skills. However, you are not spontaneously loving, and you need to make efforts in this direction. Take time out to hug your children. Although by nature you are sparing in your praise, remember that children need to have their efforts noticed and appreciated.

Libra (Sept. 24-Oct. 23): A sense of fair play, and generously given affection, mark your attitude toward your children. Cooperation is one of the keynotes of your personality. You respect your children's rights, and want to teach them to be equally respectful of yours. Harmony in the home is your foremost desire. It is toward this end that you are constantly working. You are always on hand to make sure that the little one does not damage your older children's possessions, and they in turn do not bully the baby. You have a great deal of patience, and solve family fracases tactfully and fairly.

Lucky indeed is the child whose father is a native of Libra, for he can be sure there will always be an interested ear, and wise advice to aid him in the difficult problem of growing up. This parent has the ability to discipline softly, for his charm makes him persuasive. The Libra mother, too, does not have to nag to make her point. She has a quiet authority.

Although Libra is not a fertile sign, and you rarely have very large families, you may be sure that your children will grow up happy, and be a credit to you in their adulthood. You fully know that the seeds you sow now will be reaped later, and so you show love, appreciation, and patience with your children.

Scorpio (Oct. 24-Nov. 22): Although you Scorpions usually have large families, the rearing of children is not natural to you. All human relationships are something of a strain to you. Dominant, possessive, you can be quite insistent upon having your own way. This is always a problem in a home. You are conscious of always having to curb your sharp tongue, and your need to be obeyed unquestionably presents problems.

However overbearing you may be, though, you are always

loyal to your own, and take pride in your children. You want them to excel. Your own ambition is boundless, and you pass this along to your children. You will not allow any of their talents and abilities to lie fallow. Rather, you will spend endless hours encouraging your offspring. Scorpio parents are very passionate, and although the expression of their love is harsher than that of natives of other signs, their children sense that they are deeply cared for. This security stands them in good stead.

A Scorpio parent is a tower of strength to a child in times of stress. He meets every problem with great courage and decision. Furthermore, because these natives are able to understand life perhaps better than any others, they can be extremely sympathetic and understanding.

Scorpio mothers have to cultivate gentleness and patience. Scorpio fathers need to be careful not to become the autocrats of the breakfast table. Remember that children flourish in a secure, serene home, free of strain and struggle. Compromise—and parenthood can be indeed a joy to you.

Sagittarius (Nov. 23-Dec. 22): Sagittarian parents tend to get along best with their children when their offspring are no longer babies. As a native of this sign, you are lively, active and full of fun, and enjoy your children when they become companions to you. The Sagittarius mother is likely to take her children along with her on her excursions, because she enjoys their company. Her children, in turn, are drawn to her because she transmits her love of life to them. The Sagittarius father loves the outdoors, and will take the time to teach his children sports.

You have a youthful outlook on life, and so can understand your children. Because of your almost astonishing energy, the rigors of parenthood do not exhaust you, as they do your less vigorous brothers and sisters. Because you enjoy people, your home is often the meeting place for the neighborhood children. A Sagittarius mother is likely to be den mother to her son's Boy Scout group. She can invent projects to entertain them during rainy days, and will put up with a good deal of noise and mess when the children entertain their friends.

YOU AND YOUR CHILDREN

The son of a Sagittarius mother we knew summed up his mom's attitude very well, when he said, "She's always been a pal to me. I couldn't tell her my secrets, though, in spite of this, because she's such a frank and open person she couldn't understand that I needed privacy, sometimes." So here is a danger the Sagittarius parent must avoid. Your children may resent your very honesty, sometimes. Remember that adolescence, particularly, is a sensitive time for a youngster; respect his confidences, and sympathize with his problems, even though they may not seem to you as important as he thinks they are.

Capricorn (Dec. 23-Jan. 20): Capricorn parents believe in firmness, routine and discipline. Though they temper their orders with love, they are adamant about being obeyed. However, they are devoted and self-sacrificing parents, with strong domestic and family instincts, and their children react to them with affection and a great deal of respect.

Capricorn people are "doers," and not theorists. They are less concerned with psychology books and experimental methods than they are in simple, practical measures. It was a Capricorn mother who joked that the child psychology book came in very handy; it was just the right weight to spank her son with!

Capricorn women run neat, efficient households, and take good care of their children's health and welfare. The Capricorn father is willing to lend a hand with projects and homework, and conveys his sense of routine and organization to his children. Because this is a thrifty sign, these parents are firm about waste and wanton destructiveness. "Eat it up, wear it out, make it do, or do without" is your slogan, Capricorn, and this is what you teach your children.

Family ties are important to natives of this sign. They teach their children the importance and pleasures of family gatherings, of remembering birthdays and anniversaries. There is nothing more pleasant to a Capricornian father or mother than the gathering of the clan at Christmas or Thanksgiving.

In practical matters, there is no better parent than the Capricornian. However, in matters of the heart and spirit, there may be some problems. These natives may lack the humorous, whimsical side that parents born under other stars find so helpful in enjoying their children. They need to abandon the "life is real, life is earnest" philosophy occassionally, and relax and laugh with their children. Furthermore, they have to take special pains to see that in correcting their children's behavior they do not slip into the habit of carping criticism. They must avoid setting up unnecessary restrictions, or discipline for the sake of discipline. Learn to be a bit more permissive. Remember that raising children is not only a proud responsibility, but a good deal of fun, as well!

Aquarius (Jan. 21-Feb. 19): Since Aquarius is the sign of the future, and all things modern and progressive are ruled by it, one would assume that children, who certainly belong to the future, would be Aquarius' natural forte. However, this is not always so. Aquarius people are not naturally demonstrative, and this innate aloofness presents some difficulties in dealing with their offspring.

The Aquarius mother is interested not only in her own domestic circle, but in all humanity. She is tolerant, broadminded, community-spirited. She may be the moving force in the P.T.A., or the parent who gives up every afternoon to guard the school crossings. She is likely to be a worker for causes, and her children will learn this interest in people, and sense of brotherly love, from her.

Aquarian fathers are often hobbyists. Happy indeed is the boy whose father will undertake to teach him the pleasures of handicrafts, of boating, or fishing or machine work. Humorous, friendly, this parent is always in demand as a companion.

The child of Aquarian parents is lucky in that he can always be sure of a confidante. Natives of this sign are not easily shocked. Furthermore, because they take a large view, they can usually reassure children about little problems that loom up frighteningly in a child's life. It was an Aquarian friend of the family who took the time to cure this writer's childhood fear of the dark, by explaining just why there were shadows on the wall and, unexplained noises during the night!

If an Aquarian parent can remember that children need to feel they are the center of their parents' world, and there will be time for adult interests after the children are grown, he can be both an outstanding parent and a real friend to his children.

Pisces (Feb. 20-March 21): Piscean parents adore their children, and often spoil them, for it is difficult for them to discipline their offspring. The Piscean mother is particularly partial to her youngest baby, and will joyfully cuddle him for hours on end. Since natives of this sign are by nature self-sacrificing and giving, no effort is too large for them to make. These mothers rarely whine that their children tie them down. They do not resent the thousand little demands that children make; on the contrary, "doing for" the children is a great pleasure.

Piscean natives are perhaps the most sensitive and understanding people in the Zodiac. Their children will always find a ready ear for their confidences. These parents are vitally interested in their children's emotional well-being. They are particularly effective during their offsprings' adolescence, for they readily sympathize with the lack of self-confidence and shyness that this age brings.

Although they are not materialistic, it is the Piscean parent who will say, "I want my children to have everything I missed as a child." They are likely to spin dreams over their children, envisioning them as recipients of every joy and honor the parents themselves missed. It is not so much that they are personally ambitious for their youngsters, for they do not seek glory. It is rather that they want their children to have easy and pleasant lives, and to be spared the rigors that the parents themselves may have endured.

Piscean parents are blessed, by nature, with a natural aptitude for raising children. However, they do have to be sure that they are not so easy and permissive that their children "walk all over" them. They have to remember that children not only need, but

want and respect, discipline. Keeping this in mind, Piscean
natives make excellent parents.

Your Children

Shakespeare divided the ages of man into seven, but it was
left for Gesell, Ilg and Spock to categorize the ages of children!
The resultant books have been of priceless value to parents, all
of whom must have felt that their children's problems were not
only unique, but also unsolvable!

The experts tell us that children need not only the material
necessities of life, food, shelter, clothing, but intangibles, as
well. From the carefully prescribed "by the clock" routine of
the past generation, we have progressed to a more permissive
schedule in raising babies today. Parents are told to relax
schedules, and follow more the needs of the infant. No longer is
the baby fed only at prescribed hours, instead, he is often fed
when he is hungry. Parents, a generation ago, were told to let
the baby "cry it out." Today infants are given the cuddling and
attention they need, with the understanding that it is not love
and attention, but indifference, that spoils the child!

Psychologists tell us that the child's personality is formed
far earlier than we had once thought. Some set the age as young
as four, others at seven or nine. However, they are in agreement
that the formative years are early, and that parents need to
establish the feeling of security in their youngsters from the
start. The needs of the child, *affection, understanding, approval
without condition,* must be met. Youngsters need to feel that
they are accepted for what they are, not for what they do, and
that although Mommy and Daddy may not like certain types
of behavior, they still love their children.

But a child needs standards, too. He needs to learn to respect
his own property, and the property and rights of others. He
needs to learn to share, to compromise, to sympathize. He must
learn that his chores must be carried out—even simple ones, like
putting away his toys and hanging up his clothing.

Development is more than a matter of physical growth. The child adds weight and inches, his eyes undergo changes that will enable him to read, his wrist bones develop, his muscular coordination increases, his first teeth are replaced by permanent ones. And with all these changes, comes other development, too. Between one and two he begins to walk, to respond to voices, and to speak, if only a few words. Between two and three he learns to climb stairs, to throw or kick a ball, to use blocks, to feed himself. By four he is comparatively self-sufficient. He runs, jumps, climbs, rides a tricycle. He plays with crayons and paints, enjoys being with other children, can dress and undress himself with some skill. He composes little stories, may know his address and telephone number. By five his small muscles are better developed, he can use a scissors, for instance, and saw and paint with his father. Little girls enjoy dressing up, and have "best friends."

The world is an exciting place for a six-year old, but disturbing, too, for he is "on his own" in school. His bluster hides his fears. Seven is sensitive; "It isn't my fault," he cries, for he cannot yet meet his own standards. Eight is rowdy—in fact parents have observed that the odd ages—three, five, seven and nine, are smooth, the even ones—four, six, eight and ten, are full of stress. Nine is the age of gangs and clubs, children have secrets, become interested in special fields, such as science, nature. At ten, a child is skilled at performing physical feats, enjoys gathering information, can discuss problems, reason, see both sides of an argument.

The gateway to adolescence is the door to independence. But the path is indeed rocky. The young person, caught between the desire to be cared for and protected as a child, and the wish to be a self-reliant adult, has many inner pressures. He is alternately belligerent and agreeable, aggressive and sensitive. He has periodic bouts of rebellion that may bewilder his family, but are his way of asserting his coming manhood.

The parents' way through this maze of growth is not an easy one. A comedian joked, "With one slap, my father wiped out eight stages"; This may present one solution, but not always the happiest one. It would be fine, indeed, if there were a magic formula by which we could develop to the full our children's inborn abilities. But there is none. Perhaps the following paragraphs may shed some light on the personalities of your children, and help you as parents to understand them, and to understand how you can best influence their behavior to help them reach happy, useful maturity.

Aries (March 22-Apr. 20): The Aries child is a handful! In fact, this is true of all children born in the Spring—Taurus and Gemini as well. Like the season itself, these children are alternately sunny and stormy, exuberant and full of life. Aries children are usually good looking, and are charming, likeable little people. They have good dispositions, and are generous and friendly.

Young Ariens are early talkers and walkers, and in fact, tend toward precocity. They have a tremendous curiosity, and seem to always be asking "why?". The Aries determination and courage show at an early age. It is necessary for the parents to lead these children, rather than to push them. They are very independent. Try to avoid "power struggles" with them.

These first-sign natives can excel in school, if their interest is kindled. They dislike detail work. They prefer activities that allow them to exploit their lively imaginations. The Aries child usually has some project in the works. They also enjoy and are good at sports, provided they take the time to learn the fundamentals, first. They do not like to have to practice anything, for they are naturally impatient.

Parents of Aries youngsters need to remember that although these children show signs of self-sufficiency very early, they are much more in need of affection, guidance and care than they indicate. They are inwardly sensitive, although a brash exterior hides this quality. They need to be allowed to vent their creative urges. Naturally honest, they should be trusted, and given opportunities to show their ability to handle responsibility.

Last, but not least, parents of these children should be warned that these youngsters are plagued with unusually stormy periods of adolescence, but that this does not indicate that they will be unstable adults. On the contrary, once a parent has reared his Aries son or daughter through this period, he can look forward to being able to take pride in a competent, successful and well-liked young adult.

Taurus (Apr. 21-May 21): Taurus children are lovable and loving. They adore being petted; even that cowlicky, freckled little terror will crawl up on Mommy's lap unexpectedly to get a welcome kiss! The little girls are born flirts; from earliest infancy, the Taurean miss is Daddy's girl!

The true Taurean is a solid citizen, and the children give early evidence of this. The little boy who is "all boy," and the little girl whose dolls are the best-cared-for, are likely to be born under this second sign. They are active, athletic, and on the whole, healthy.

These children are, like the adults of this sign, very competent. They arrange to do their tasks methodically, are industrious, and have good concentration. They enjoy doing things with their hands, and are very handy. This sign rules music; many children born under it show early talent in this direction. Parents who have noticed that their little Taureans keep time to the rhythm of a song, or hum and sing on key, should encourage their youngsters to take lessons, for music is a great source of pleasure to a Taurus native.

Taurus children learn slowly, but they learn thoroughly. They should not be rushed, for then they rebel. Like the turtle in the story, Taurean children find that "slow but steady wins the race."

It is easy to err when raising a Taurean youngster. They seem so sturdy and self-reliant that it is hard to believe they need a great deal of love and praise. Do not challenge a child born under this sign; he becomes belligerent, stubborn, and, like the elephant, does not forget. A Taurean child who has been badly handled, and denied the affection and attention that are his birthright withdraws into himself, and becomes difficult, if not impossible, to reach. Treat these little boys and girls with approval, and love, and they respond like flowers to the sun.

Gemini (May 22-June 21): "Even when I know she's bent on mischief, I can't stop her," the mother of a Gemini youngster wailed. "She's so fast!" Of course she is; she is like the Mercury that rules this sign. It is all the parent of a Gemini child can do to keep this youngster in sight!

Gemini children are a mixed joy and trial. They are active, lithe, graceful, have considerable charm and ability. They usually are adept in anything they do; they read well and early, are mechanically inclined, are creative and artistic, and have no trouble expressing themselves verbally. In fact, many a mother of a Gemini child, stuck in with him on a rainy day, finds herself talked out to the point of exhaustion midway through the afternoon!

The trick with a Gemini child is to keep him busy, or better still, to provide plenty of material for his active imagination to employ, so that he can plan his own projects. Gemini's mind works day and night. Care has to be taken in handling these youngsters, for they are inclined to be nervous and high-strung. Eventually they will have to learn concentration and system, but parents in teaching this, must not be dogmatic.

It is very important to be completely honest with these youngsters. They sense a lie immediately. They cannot be forced into anything that seems unethical to them. A point to remember in dealing with a Gemini child is that because he lives in a world of imagination, he may appear to be telling tall tales. However, to a Gemini native, fantasy is often the real truth.

Cancer (June 22-July 23): Perhaps more than the children of any other sign, Cancer children have deep emotional needs. The strongest influence on a Cancerian is always his own home environment, and Cancer children react tremendously to their parents and siblings. They may be too shy to express their desires, but they want to be made much of.

These little boys and girls are likely to be manageable children. They tend to rebel in adolescence, but, as little ones, they do not need a great deal of discipline. All Cancerians have strong inner lives; these children can sit and play quietly by themselves for hours at a time. The little girls enjoy helping with the cooking, and the boys are usually close to their mothers. The mother of a Cancerian little boy may worry that he is too tightly tied to her apron strings, but this trait will provide the background for his future ability to form a loving attachment to his own wife and children.

Cancer children are moody, particularly in their teens. They are very sensitive, and sometimes imagine hurts and slights where none exist. There is an old adage that says, "The squeaky wheel gets the grease." Just because Cancer children rarely "squeak," it is easy to overlook their problems and tribulations. However, it cannot be overemphasized that this must be avoided. These children require a great deal of emotional understanding and attention. Denied this, their fine, loving, sympathetic natures become stunted, and their natural compassion turns into silent brooding and self-pity.

Leo (July 24-Aug. 23): A Leo man tells of the time he, as a boy, was taken to the circus with a group of his friends. "I ate two bags of peanuts, *shells and all,*" he laughs, "to get attention." No wonder—a three-ring circus is heavy competition to the limelight-loving Leo!

Leo children are leaders, and leaders in the very best sense of the word. They invent games and activities, and in general are very constructive in group play. They are liked and respected by their playmates, for they have a self-confidence that shows itself from the time they are toddlers.

Leo children love parties and clubs. They have a real flair for the dramatic. It is the Leo youngster who operates the puppet shows and gives plays in his backyard to entertain his friends. Very romance-conscious, they have early crushes. The teen-aged girl whose telephone rings from early til late, is likely to be a Leo.

Leo is a noble sign. There is much to be proud of for the parent whose youngster is a native of Leo. However, these children have a tendency to be somewhat autocratic, and can rule the roost if given a chance. Parents need to remember that children do not really want to dominate the household. They know they are not equipped to make adult decisions. It is necessary for their sense of security to know that it is the parents who set the domestic pace.

Virgo (Aug. 24-*Sept.* 23): A parent of a tiny Virgo baby made this observation recently: "Even though she can't say a word yet, she listens intently and tries to imitate every sound she hears." This is a true Virgo characteristic for Virgo's ruler, Mercury, has rulership over speech. Virgo children are early and fluent talkers. In fact, they seem strangely adult at a very young age, and are companionable even as toddlers.

Raising a Virgo child is likely to be a very pleasant experience. They are usually neat and orderly. They take care to put away their toys when they are finished with them. In school they exhibit good conduct, and learn rapidly. They are not often "troublesome" in any way, except that they are inclined to be picky eaters.

The true Virgo native is a highly efficient person. He is accurate with detail work, and has a highly critical sense which manifests itself in childhood. These youngsters are very adaptable. They have good dispositions, though they are sensitive and sometimes rather shy. A Virgo adolescent suffers a great deal. A man we know, born under this sign, told of his first love, a high school classmate of his, whom he never had the courage to ask for a date! In the same way, even very pretty Virgo girls are certain that they are not liked by boys, and cannot be convinced that their demure ways are indeed very charming.

Parents of Virgo children, like those of Geminian youngsters, need to have on hand a good deal of play and educational material. Virgo children enjoy education, and by and large, if they miss it during their youth, will regret it very much later on.

Lessons in special subjects, books, and if possible, a college education, are things that the parents of these youngsters should make every effort to provide.

Libra (Sept. 24-Oct. 23): Few people can resist Libra children for they are usually beautiful, amiable and loving. Pollyana, the little girl whose sunny disposition was an uplifting force to the adults around her, must have been a Libra native.

Libra children are cooperative, easy to get along with. Calm and balanced, they do not seem to pass through as extreme stages as do other children. Even as adolescents, they are graceful, pleasant, and charming.

These children may seem to be self-indulgent, to people who do not know the need a Libran has for peace, harmony and comfort. The parent of a young Libra miss complained that this teen-age girl drove the family wild by tying up the bathroom for two-hour bubble baths! Friends tried to tell her that this is a mild manifestation of a difficult age, and that many mothers would gladly settle for this type of behavior!

Libra natives tend to early marriages, and even as children are very much aware of the opposite sex. These youngsters may even pair off and go steady when they are scarcely past childhood. In all their dealings with their friends, they create little friction. They get along well, for it is easy for them to compromise. A Libran is rarely a rebel, and even when he has a cause, he is so gentle and persuasive that he easily wins his points. Parents of these children should have the welcome mat dusted off, for the child will have a host of friends.

Oddly enough, it is because of the charm and diplomacy that is natural to members of this sign, that problems arise. These children may find that it is easy to coast through life, without really making an effort. Because their teachers like them, they can get away with school work that does not represent really hard work. They may find it is easier to avoid discord than it is to take a stand on an issue. Parents need to encourage these children to seek ideals, and to defend them, for a life of compromise

can make one spineless and lacking in direction. Libra children
need to be made aware that character can never be attained by
dreaming, but must be forged and hammered out of life.

Scorpio (Oct. 24-Nov. 22): "There was a little girl, who had a
little curl, right in the middle of her forehead. When she was
good, she was very, very good, and when she was bad, she was
horrid!" There—that sums up the Scorpio child!

Scorpio is said to be the strongest sign of the Zodiac. At any
rate, it is certainly true that being the parent of a child born
under this sign is not easy! Before listing the pitfalls, astrologers
do say that there are two sides to the Scorpio nature, and it is
generally true that it is the more negative one that appears in
childhood. With good training, these traits can be modified,
and this accomplished, the positive side will shine through.
Remember, the higher type of Scorpion is one of the most
admirable members of the Zodiacal family.

Strong is a Scorpio word! These children have strong physiques,
and even stronger wills! They enjoy nothing more than a good
fight, and they usually win. Compromise is hard for them; even
when they give the appearance of giving in, they are marking
time until they can again revive the fracas. They have violent
tempers, and intense likes and dislikes.

Scorpio children are wise beyond their years. They are quick
to ferret out secrets, and are early blessed with a great deal of
instinctive understanding of others. They have powerful intel-
lects, and if they choose, can be outstanding students. Plain-
spoken, inclined to sarcasm, they seem to be direct, but behind
it there is a strong need for privacy and secrecy. These children
should be permitted to have a locked drawer. A diary with a lock
is a perfect gift for a Scorpio girl.

It is not easy to discourage a Scorpio youngster, nor to deter
him from whatever path he may choose. It is important to
impress upon him the qualities of honesty, courtesy, and consideration for others. He must be taught to overcome the drives
that can despoil his character. With their fine minds and mag-

netic personalities, these children have a potential which must not be allowed to go unrealized.

The parent of a Scorpio child has his work cut out for him! But if he can give consistent and wise discipline, and a great deal of love to this child, he will reap the rewards. There is no greater challenge to a parent!

Sagittarius (Nov. 23-Dec. 22): The familiar calendar picture of a blue-jeaned little boy carrying a can of worms, as he goes fishing, his mongrel puppy following close behind him, must have been inspired by a little Sagittarian. These children are fond of the outdoors, and sports, and adore animals. Parents must remember never to deprive a Sagittarian child of the pleasure of a pet. They also enjoy activities that are connected with animals, such as horseback riding.

Sagittarian children enjoy strenuous activity, and are equipped for it by nature, for they have strong bodies and are usually healthy. The only problem that parents generally encounter with these youngsters, is that they are sometimes reckless in sports, and are prone to injury. Aside from that, they are vigorous and sound.

Children born under this sign are winning little creatures. They are frank and outspoken, have good senses of humor, and are popular both with their contemporaries and adults. Even in adolescence they are not often given to the brooding moods that are common at that period of life. Nothing is undercover with a native of this sign. From earliest childhood, what is on their minds is on their tongues. They dislike injustice and intolerance, and will not stand for deceit.

Sagittarius children are often good scholars, for they are naturally bright and alert. Furthermore, they enjoy learning. However, they find detail work boring, and a school program that relies heavily on drill and memorization will fail to bring out the best in them. They do not like to have to sit still for long, and get uneasy in any situation where they are not allowed freedom of motion. Parents must learn to make allowances for this restlessness, for it is a sign of an eager, many-faceted intelligence.

Youngsters born under this sign have a predisposition toward religion. Later in life they may not be interested in the church, for they are basically students of humanity rather than lovers of dogma, but as children, they have a striving toward God. Their parents should provide books and material on religion, and make it possible for them to go to Sunday School.

An important point to be remembered in rearing a Sagittarian child, is that he must be permitted a great deal of freedom. He hates restrictions, and cannot develop into his best self under limitations. He wants to be independent right from the beginning. Do not try to supervise him, if you can avoid it. Trust him, instead. Let him know you have faith in him, and his strong sense of honor will take over.

Another hint: it is sometimes hard to develop a good understanding of thrift and prudence in a Sagittarian child. It might be a good plan to put him on an allowance, and let him learn early how to manage money. Sagittarius people have a tendency to be extravagant, and it is a wise idea to curb this early in life.

Capricorn (Dec. 23-Jan. 20): It is said of Capricorn that he is old in his youth, and young in his old age! It is certainly true that the self-contained little Capricornian telling her mother, "You be the baby and I'll be the Mommy," gives every indication of being able to handle the adult role very effectively! They are born with an innate sense of dignity, and seem, right from the beginning, to be able to handle themselves.

Capricorn children know early what they want out of life. They are definite in their tastes, strong-willed, and ambitious. They are not given to wavering or wishful thinking. They have less interest in childish pranks or histrionics than do natives of other signs. Generally they are good students, particularly once they master the fundamentals. They do not always learn quickly, but they are thorough. They have great powers of concentration. Moreover, they hate slovenliness and laziness. They are rarely satisfied with their own efforts, however, and may tend to get discouraged if the task is really too far above their years.

These youngsters do not like to have hordes of friends. They prefer to have a few close companions, or even one "best friend." They are very happy in the bosom of their families, and usually grow up with a strong respect for their families. They enjoy outings with relatives more than social activities with outsiders.

As with all the earth sign natives, Virgo, Taurus and Capricorn, the children are not fast starters. Youngsters of other signs show more promise in childhood, but Capricorn natives win out, for they have the determination and the courage in the face of heavy odds that brings ultimate success. These qualities of character take time to develop, but they are the most important ones in the long run.

Aquarius (Jan. 21-*Feb.* 19): "I know every mother thinks her child is unusual," the parent of an Aquarian child confessed, "but Johnny is so different from the rest of the family that we can't make head or tails of him!" And she is right, too, for an Aquarian child *is* unique. His day-dreams may be unfathomable, for his mind is occupied with a reality that does not concern the average child. His philosophic outlook is inborn, and shows itself when he is very young.

The Aquarian child may seem hard to reach, for he has a way of shutting out unpleasant reality. His mind is always at work on some unusual idea. He is quick and intelligent, eager to learn, but impatient of routine and detail. A problem is that although he enjoys praise and recognition, he does not always work toward that goal. He may find his fantasies as satisfying as real achievement.

Aquarian children have an equal need for both company and for solitude. They are popular, for people respect them. Natives of this sign are often the officers in school government. They are friends well worth having, for they give freely of themselves. They are tolerant, understanding, and loyal. They brook no criticism of their friends or families. On the other hand, they also have a deep desire to be alone. They are rarely bored with their own company. They enjoy hobbies, are inventive, and usually have a project "in the works." The toddler who can stay in his room for hours, playing quietly with his toys, is probably a little Aquarian.

Youngsters born under this sign are determined, and generally get their own way, although they do not make much noise about it. The approach they use is tactful, but there is little use in bucking an Aquarian child. Although he seems to compromise, in the end *his* will is done.

Aquarian children should be treated as equals, whenever possible. They very much resent being talked down to. They are sensitive to punishment, and unsympathetic treatment will cause them to retreat into a hard shell and become unapproachable. Although they are fixed in their ways, even as youngsters, they can be reasoned with. If they are guilty of unacceptable behavior, they should be corrected *quietly*. They are usually able to see the error of their ways, and will discipline themselves. They dislike being criticized, but will take suggestions, if tactfully presented. A parent, in dealing with these children, should remember that this sun-sign bestows a tremendous potential, and that patience and understanding will pay off.

Pisces (Feb. 20-*March* 21): Anthony Armstrong-Jones, husband of Princess Margaret Rose of England, is a Piscean. In describing his childhood, his stepmother says that he could always get his way, not by giving orders or throwing tantrums, but by adeptly charming others to do his bidding.

Another story she tells is about his favorite activity—amateur theatrics—in which he played Peter Pan, a role in which, by means of a ceiling pulley, he was able to fly through the air! Piscean children live in a world of fantasy, and particularly enjoy anything that is far from the everyday patterns and routines.

It is sometimes difficult for even the wisest parent to understand the child born under the sign of Pisces. This youngster seems to have a dual nature. On the one hand he is honest, conscientious and trustworthy. On the other, he is given to moods of mystery and withdrawal. A point to remember is that these youngsters, like all children, need to be noticed and appreciated, but Piscean natives also require a great deal of privacy. In fact, many a mother has noticed that halfway through a conversation with her Piscean child, she is looking into a blank countenance. The child's mind is a million miles away, and he is in his own secret world!

Most children born under this sign are artistic, and many are particularly talented in the fields of music and dance. They enjoy reading, although they may not have the concentration required for heavy material. They are good storytellers, and may enjoy writing little tales and poems. They are sympathetic companions; even when they are little they show mature wisdom and understanding. Most of these youngsters enjoy the company of adults more than of other children.

Natives of this sign are among the most sensitive people in the Zodiac. A chiding remark made lightly may leave a scar that lasts for years. They become enraged when a confidence is betrayed. Although these children are amiable when they are little, they frequently have difficult adolescences. The quiet little girl who suddenly turns "boy crazy" as a teenager, or the boy who becomes a "rebel without a cause," is likely to be a native of this sign. However, these are passing phases. More likely than not, these young people will turn into serene adults, bolstered by a strong intellectual and artistic bent. The parents can aid them in achieving productive adulthood by remembering that Pisces natives need much encouragement in order to believe in themselves. More than any other sign, these youngsters react badly to nagging criticism. They must be handled gently, for their egos are easily bruised.

VI. Astrology is
Your Best Medicine

IF you owned Aladdin's lamp, what would be your three wishes? Your second and third wish might be for wealth, for beauty, for adventure, love, fame or recognition. But the first, without a doubt, would be for good health. For without this greatest of all blessings, all other fortune would be useless.

Ours is called the age of anxiety. The figures showing the amounts of money spent annually on "happy pills," painkillers, sleeping potions, stomach palliatives and other drugs, are truly staggering. And yet, if most of us were to observe simple rules for good health we could save ourselves much distress. Good health is not only a gift of God, it is a goal that is within the reach of many of us, as well.

This is not a chapter about medicine. The only advice that can be safely given to one who is taken ill, is that he see a physician, immediately. In fact, it goes without saying, that it is wise to have periodic medical check-ups, regardless of the state of your health. Rather, it is our purpose to suggest that by using "preventative medicine," it is possible to keep fit, and to add years to your life, each one filled with zest and pleasure.

Tiberius, the wise Roman emperor, defined good hygiene. "Use three physicians:" he wrote, "First, Doctor Quiet; then Doctor Diet; and then, Doctor Merryman." Long before the age of popular psychiatry and calory-counting, this sage knew that moderation in all things, good food habits, and proper rest and recreation are the secrets of health. So, with him, let us visit these three physicians, and see what their prescriptions are! Dr. Quiet is the most elusive. If you are one of those lucky individuals who can lean back in your chair, close your eyes, and drift off into refreshing sleep, you don't need any advice. Teddy Roosevelt was one of those fortunate people, and so was Napoleon, who was said to have been able to sleep on horseback! Thomas Edison advocated only four hours sleep a night, but he was a cat-napper, who found it easy to recharge his batteries by sleeping frequently during the day, for short periods of time. However, most of us, at least at one time or another in our lives, have some difficulty getting enough sleep.

Doctors tell us that the most common causes of sleeplessness are: worries about the future, and concern about our own faults and shortcomings. Insomnia may be due to frustration, or it may be due to mild indigestion. However, whatever the causes, here is what the experts tell us:

First, do not worry about a loss of sleep. There is no set number of hours necessary. If you lose a night's sleep, your body will recoup the following night. Insomnia itself is not dangerous; it is the worrying about it that is devastating.

Secondly, practice a steady bedtime routine. Have a regular bedtime hour. Try a warm bath, mild limbering exercise, or a hot drink (not coffee, or any other stimulant, of course). Once in bed, avoid the temptation to switch positions, looking for the one that is the most comfortable. Lie quietly; it is hard to stay awake when you are in one position for some time. Check your room for too much noise or light, and make sure that bedclothes, pajamas, etc., are comfortable. Do not count sheep, or play any mental games. Most important, make your mind blank when you begin to rehash the day's mistakes, or worry about the morrow.

As important as a good night's sleep, is rest during the day. If it is possible to take a nap after lunch, as Winston Churchill and Harry Truman always do, grab the opportunity. You will find you are refreshed for the remainder of the day and evening. Tests on students at Stephens College proved that the group who rested after lunch were able to do their work considerably better than those who were active. Doctors advise the mothers of young children to resist the temptation to catch up on their work while the children are napping, but rather to lie down during these quiet times.

Doctor Diet is today's most popular practitioner. Never before have so many been worried about their weight! Statistics compiled by life-insurance companies show that in this land of plenty, far too many of us are overweight. The life span, they have found, is directly related to weight. The healthiest men and women, it seems, have weights slightly below the average. The life expectancy of an individual falls off sharply with every pound of excess weight. For this reason, it is desirable to restrict the diet to health-giving foods, and to go lightly on the fattening sweets and starches that many of us prefer.

Of all the advice concerning diet that comes down through the ages, the most often repeated is—moderation! "Eat to live, don't live to eat" is the correct attitude.

Dr. Diet may sometimes prescribe some rather bitter medicine, but Doctor Merryman offers nothing but fun. In fact, fun is the whole point. In the words of the song, he suggests you "try a little happiness." Friends, hobbies, sports and vacations are in Doctor Merryman's domain. Elsewhere in this book, there are sections on vacations and sports under the heading, "Your Leisure Time." Judicious use of recreation can pay off in terms of health and happiness.

Now, what does astrology have to do with your health? Astromedicine, the science of diagnosing and prescribing, on the basis of horoscopes, is one of the oldest uses of astrology. History shows us that the ancients used this method almost exclusively. Throughout the ages, dominion over various organs in the body have been given to certain stars and planets. The following sections of the body have been ascribed to these signs:

Aries:	Head and face
Taurus:	Throat and neck
Gemini:	Shoulders, arms and hands

Cancer:	Stomach, breast and lungs
Leo:	Back, heart, liver
Virgo:	Lower abdomen, intestines
Libra:	Kidney, bladder, nerves
Scorpio:	Groin, spine
Sagittarius:	Hips, joints, thighs
Capricorn:	Knees, skin, bony structure
Aquarius:	Lower leg, calves, ankles
Pisces:	Feet, arches, toes

These classifications do not, of course, mean that if you were born while the sun was in Pisces, you are doomed to a lifetime of flat feet, or if you have Aries prominent in your chart, you will suffer from headaches, any more than if you have no relationship to Leo, you are guaranteed never to have heart trouble. There are many aspects, too numerous to explain fully in this chapter, that indicate health or illness in a chart.

However, astrologers have found that there are certain weak points in each horoscope, as well as indications of strength. For instance, active, nervous Ariens, by virtue of their metabolistic make-up, are often subject to a different variety of ailments than are the more phlegmatic Taureans.

With the following paragraphs serving only as a guide, find the description of your state of health. And again, remember that most of us are a composite of several signs; our horoscopes show a diversity of planet distribution, containing both good and bad aspects to the sixth house, which is the house of health.

Most important, do not forget that these hints that astrology gives you are not meant to take the place of competent medical advice. Rather, they serve as a guide to help you take precautions in the areas in which you are most likely to encounter difficulties. Again, if you have any specific symptoms or illnesses—see your doctor.

Aries (March 22-April 20): If you are a typical Arien, you probably enjoy very good health. Active and energetic, you have a hatred for physical infirmity. In fact, one of your problems, is that you tend to ignore symptoms, thinking that if you don't pay any attention to them, they will go away! And it is a good thing you are naturally robust, for you are a terrible patient! You have no interest in following the doctor's directions. Deep down, you are convinced that you know more than he does, anyway! If you are told to rest in bed for several days, the chances are you will be off and running about the first day.

"Pep" is an Aries word. You are given to great spurts of energy. Long past the point of physical exhaustion, you are still carrying on. "I have two states of being," an Aries woman explained. "I either feel just wonderful, or else I am at the point of physical collapse!" A track star, who happened to be a native of this sign, explained his success. "When I feel I can't go on, that is the time when I begin to sprint."

Your sign rules the head and face, and also, by opposition, the nerves and kidneys. You may be one of the natives of this sign who explains that he doesn't mind visits to the doctor, but dreads those sessions with the dentist. Your sign rules the teeth, and you must be sure you do not skip those important dental check-ups.

As youngsters, you Ariens are particularly prone to accidents, especially those that damage the head and face. All Ariens enjoy sports in which there is an element of risk, and so have to exercise particular care to avoid injury.

A simple diet, with an emphasis on vegetables and fruits, is usually best for you fire-sign natives. You must also watch that you do not overwork, for breakdowns are a great danger. Many of you don't know when to stop to rest. You do not like to admit that you require much sleep, but you are so active that you must rest, in order to recapture your strength.

The greatest danger you face, is that you may have difficulty controlling your emotions, and so are at the mercy of the ravages of anger, excitement and worry. You tend to overtax your strength. In spite of your energy, you have little staying power.

Learn not to drive yourself too hard, and avoid over-eating and excessive use of alcohol. Yours is a healthy sign, by and large, and if you treat your body kindly, it can retain its youthful vigor for many years.

Taurus (Apr. 21-May 21): The mellow voice of Bing Crosby, a Taurean, has been said to be caused by—of all things—nodes on his larynx! Here is an interesting example of how a birthchart can bring not only problems but blessings. Taurus rules the larynx, as well as the rest of the throat.

Generally speaking, the neck and throat are weak points for you second-sign people. As a native of this sign, you should be especially sure to wear a scarf when the weather is cold, and to protect yourself from drafts that may cause a stiff neck. You have probably noticed that when you catch a cold, it tends to settle in this area, or in the bronchial tubes. Laryngitis is an ailment that may plague you.

By and large, you are naturally healthy and robust. You have real brute strength, and rarely seem to become fatigued. Your staying power, in contrast to that of your Aries brothers and sisters, for instance, is great. You dislike admitting that you do not feel well. Hypochondria is not likely to be a Taurus shortcoming, particularly for the men of this sign. Unfortunately, however, partly because you do not heed the early warnings of illness, and partly because of your physical make-up, you often recover slowly from illness.

Taurus natives are fine patients. They can stand up to pain and discomfort better than most, and do not give in to fear. Furthermore, they will follow doctor's directions, and take the treatments prescribed, no matter how unpleasant. They do not have a "wise guy" attitude about their health.

Typically, natives of this sign are solidly built, and stocky. The true Taurean male is muscular, large-shouldered, and has strong arms and chest. The women are not tall, but are rather voluptuously built, with beautiful clear skin and healthy hair. Queen Elizabeth II of England is a very good example of Taurean looks. Unhappily, both sexes tend to gain weight later in life. They must exercise particular caution when it comes to diet, for they are partial to rich, well-flavored food. Physical activity, with emphasis upon such exercise as walking, gardening and swimming, should be a part of the daily routine. Remember, it is easier to keep in trim than it is to try to overcome the ill-effects of indiscriminate living.

Gemini (May 22-June 21): Stephen Leacock's man who mounted his horse and rode off madly in all directions at once, must have been a native of Gemini! Nervous and active, you Geminians try to accomplish too much, and wear yourselves out in the process. Insomnia can be a problem for you; you find it difficult to relax, even when you are exhausted. Your mind is always alert; you are prone to fretting and worrying.

If you are a typical Geminian, you are slim and rather delicately built, with long arms and legs, and fine, dry skin, which is sensitive. In general, natives of your sign do not tend toward excess weight, as do those born under Taurus, for example. Of course, it must be reiterated that few people follow their astrological types exactly; most of us are a blend of several signs.

Gemini traditionally has reign over the upper chest, lungs and arms. You are apt to suffer from colds. If you are the sort of person who has one cold immediately following another, there is some chance that you may be allergic. Sensitivity to pollen, food and drugs is often found in natives of your sign. Many of you suffer from hay fever, or rose fever.

Despite your delicate appearance, and your tendency toward minor respiratory illnesses, your general health is good. You are not the sort who overindulges in food or liquor, and so your digestion is likely to be good. It is fortunate that you are in the main, rather healthy, for you are a very poor patient. Enforced rest has little charm for you. You usually have a project or two that demands your attention, and cannot take the time to spend being sick.

The major point of strain in your physique is your nerves. You must learn the art of relaxation, which is a hard lesson for you. Take up a hobby, or cultivate other forms of recreation.

Learn to put your troubles behind you at the end of each work day. Be careful about accidents; natives of your sign usually are too impatient to observe the rules of safety. You are inclined to be speedy drivers. Although you are naturally adept behind the wheel, you too can make mistakes. These precautions observed, you can enjoy the good health that is a Gemini birthright.

Cancer (June 22-July 23): A little Cancer girl, describing her idea of heaven, said wistfully, "It's a mountain of ice cream, a mile high." Here is Cancer's downfall—they love rich food! Excess weight is likely to be a real problem. If you are typical of this sign, you may have to watch your eating habits carefully all your life. It is not that you eat large quantities of food, but the type you choose is your trouble. You love sweets, pastries, starches, and calory-laden sauces, all of which, particularly after middle age, can add extra pounds. Furthermore, you do not enjoy excercise—and rich foods, plus a passive life add up to obesity.

Cancer children are rather delicate; they are prone to all the childhood diseases. However, as they grow older, they become stronger, and often develop robust health later in life. They do not take pain well, for the true native of this sign has a sensitive, highly developed nervous system.

You may have noticed that when you are calm and contented you not only feel better in your daily life, but seem to contract fewer ailments. This is particularly true of the women of this sign. Moods are important in their general health. When they are worried and depressed, they have a propensity to illness, and have a much lowered resistance. The state of mind can play havoc with one's digestion, too. Doctors tell us it is a mistake to bring our troubles with us to the dinner table. As a native of this fourth sign, try to create an oasis of quiet and peace during mealtimes, for if you eat while you are under stress, your stomach is sure to suffer.

If you are a typical Cancer native, you dislike athletics. However, exercise is an important part of good hygiene, and you should make it a point to include some in your routine, doctors claim that walking and swimming are the best sports, for all the muscles of the body are engaged during these activities. Most Cancerians enjoy water sports, fortunately. Walking can be a part of everyone's life. Even city dwellers who can't manage outdoor hikes can learn to enjoy a brisk 20-minute walk each day. This will really pay off in terms of physical well-being.

Leo (July 24-Aug. 23): "When I'm ill, I like an audience," a Leo woman confided frankly. "In fact, I even enjoyed being in the hospital! I loved the flowers, the attention from doctors and nurses, and the constant stream of visitors!" To a Leo native, everything, even illness, is a dramatic production!

If you are the typical native of Leo, you are attractive, vivacious, and have a well-shaped, strong body. You are inclined to look healthy, even when you are not feeling well, for you have high color, rosy cheeks, and bright eyes. By nature, you are robust, have a strong constitution, and recover quickly from illnesses. Of course, you may strain your physical health, for you are the hardest workers of the Zodiac, and may overwork to the point of breakdown.

Like all fire-sign natives, you are fond of outdoor activity and sports. Guard against accidents, and do not take unnecessary chances when you drive. Patience is not one of your long suits, but try to remember that it is better to spend an extra few minutes on the road than it is to take a foolish chance that may result in serious injury.

Over-indulgence may be your bugaboo. Leo natives are fond of lots of good food, and may be inclined to excessive drinking and smoking. Because you have tremendous vitality, and live life to the fullest, many temptations may be placed in your path. Live wisely, so that you may enjoy your life for many years to come.

Virgo (Aug. 24-Sept. 23): A Virgo man, whose splendid physical health is the envy of all his friends, recently let them in on a secret. His kitchen cupboard contained bottles of every vitamin pill on the market, plus jars, bottles and packages of all the latest "health foods." He was exercising typical Virgo concern about his diet. The sign rules the digestive tract, and it is here that a Virgoan's potential troubles lie. A native of this sign, more than any other, must watch his diet, and treat his digestion kindly.

In general, you, as a Virgoan, enjoy good health. You are sane and sensible in your living habits. Your ability to use good judgment in this area can enable you to add years to your life, and to enjoy good health at an advanced age.

Typically, the Virgo native is slender, well-knit, and about medium height. Your sign inclines to rather sallow skin, brown hair, high cheekbones, and a small chin. The women of this sign are often beautiful, but do not have animated expressions. Of course, the true Virgo type is a rarity, for most people are influenced by many other aspects besides their sun signs.

Experts are in agreement that exercise is necessary for the well-functioning of the body. However, Virgo natives often do not like sports, or feel that they do not have the time to spend outdoors. They are dedicated and industrious workers, and do not like to take time away from their work. By fitting some mild exercise into their busy routines, though, they will find that they benefit in increased energy, and this will more than make up for the time spent.

It is fortunate that Virgoans are rarely ill, for they are fearful of bad health. In fact, there are many hypochondriacs born under this sign. Of course, this tendency toward imaginary ailments has its positive sign, too, for natives of this sign are likely to go to doctors for frequent health check-ups. Thus they rarely let an ailment progress to the point where it is difficult or impossible to treat.

As your weak points are your stomach and nerves, you can safeguard your health by watching your diet, avoiding highly-seasoned, hard-to-digest foods, and most important, by being sure that you dine in an atmosphere of calm and quiet. Avoid worry—it is your largest problem—and balance your working day with periods of rest and recreation.

Libra (Sept. 24-Oct. 23): Because you Libra natives are so well groomed, you always appear healthy and well cared for. Looks may be deceiving, sometimes, for this seventh-sign of the Zodiac does not indicate as robust health as do some of the others. "I catch everything," may be your complaint. You do not seem to have much resistance to contagious illness. A Libra child may literally have "one cold after another" all winter. Adults of this sign may find that simple viruses lay them low for long periods of time. The cold and damp are your enemies, too; you are likely to suffer, at one time or another in your life, from sciatica, rheumatism and backaches.

The typical Libra native is well-built and good looking. The men are tall and handsome, and the women are slim, but curvaceous. The sign indicates large, beautiful eyes, a full "cupid's bow" mouth, clear complexion, and wavy hair. Rita Hayworth is an example of the Libra woman's beauty.

You, as a Libran, do not like to suffer in silence. If you are ill, you make no secret of it. You like to be cared for. You want flowers, get-well cards, and plenty of attention. Unlike the natives of your opposite sign, Aries, who are ashamed of ill health, and want to be left alone to recuperate, you prefer a great deal of sympathy. Then, too, you may find illness an escape, and want to prolong a situation in which you are buffered from the rigors of everyday life.

The most important rule for you to observe, is to be sure to get enough rest. You like to be active socially, and a round of the meetings and parties you enjoy may leave you tired, but you are reluctant to forgo the conviviality that means so much to you. Make it a point to allow yourself eight hours of sleep, and try to rest for a short while during the day, too, if it is possible.

Natives of Libra must be careful not to strain their backs. Doctors have found a correlation between sedentary work and back troubles, so if yours is a desk job, try to take some regular exercises to strengthen your back muscles. It is far easier to prevent backache than it is to cure it. Swimming is excellent therapy, and so is walking. Dancing, too, is a good workout, and is one that you popular, fun-loving people may enjoy.

Scorpio (Oct. 24-Nov. 22): In regard to your health, as well as to every other aspect of your life, you believe that you are "master of my fate." Your long suit is willpower. You feel that you can control the state of your health, simply by willing it. You have no patience with any sort of ailment or infirmity. Like Theodore Roosevelt, a Scorpion, who turned the delicate health of his youth into a vigorous maturity, you believe in all forms of strenuous exercise. You have great powers of endurance, and can triumph over a physical condition that would lay low anyone else.

If you are typical of your sign, you are thick-set, srtongly knit, and sturdy. The sign indicates large bones, a powerful jaw, and a determined mouth. The eyes tend to be piercing and cold, the eyebrows bushy. The women of this sign have a voluptuous beauty, and the men are very masculine in appearance.

It is fortunate that nature has endowed Scorpio natives with strong bodies, for these people frequently indulge in excesses that would ruin a less sturdy constitution. They tend toward overeating and drinking. Sex is ruled by Scorpio, and in this area, too, moderation and discretion must be used.

If you are a typical eighth-sign native, you tend to disregard the first warnings of illness. You do not trust doctors, and you detest bed-rest. It is a real effort for you to take any sort of curative measures, and as for periodic check-ups—the idea rarely occurs to you! If you are really sick, though, you are a good patient, for you have outstanding courage. When it comes to pain, you simply "grin and bear it."

By and large, you are strong enough to resist many of the ailments that plague your weaker brothers and sisters. If you are careful about watching for danger signals and obeying sensible rules of hygiene, you are among the longest-lived people in the Zodiac.

Sagittarius (Nov. 23-Dec. 22): With Jupiter, the planet of good fortune, as guiding star, no wonder natives of your sign are so often found to be "healthy, wealthy and wise." Good health is very important to you—for you need to be vigorous in order to lead the active life you prefer. For you, good health must be more than just an absence of disease. You need, in order to consider yourself really healthy, a state of glowing euphoria. Happily, most natives of your sign are resistant to disease, and furthermore, are sensible enough to preserve their strong constitutions by sane living.

Physically, the Sagittarian type is tall, well-developed and athletic. The men are distinguished in appearance, and the women are wholesome and attractive. Both sexes have excellent posture. In later years, natives of this sign may tend to become portly, but they rarely become flabby. Lithe and graceful Mary Martin, whose annual television portrayal of Peter Pan requires her to expend physical effort that would be tiring to even a very young girl, shows how a native of this sign is able to retain the physical strength of youth for many years.

You, as a Sagittarian, are not likely to excesses. You are fond of the simple things of life, and do not seek stimulation in liquor or in carousing until late hours. You enjoy the healthful outdoors. You prefer simple, good food to rich and exotic dishes. In short, you know how to live in order to keep fit.

On the whole, the Sagittarius personality is well-balanced, but some of you err in the direction of too much activity, and too little rest. You must take care not to scatter your energy, and to be sure you conserve your strength and vigor. Do not become involved in a round of activities that prevent you from getting enough sleep. Be on guard against overwork. You have a tendency to work by "spurts," and the pressure of this sort of life can be debilitating. Your enthusiasms carry you on to a fever-peak of excitement, so that you do not feel the strain until much later. Remember, given half a chance, your robust good health will carry you on to a healthy old age.

Capricorn (Dec. 23-Jan. 20): "Be sober and temperate, and you will be healthy," said Benjamin Franklin, voicing the Capricorn sentiment about health. Of course, the problem is that while your practical good sense may tell you how to live wisely, you may find it quite another matter to put these rules into practice!

You natives of Capricorn are not a sickly group. You get off to a poor start as youngsters, but you grow much stronger as you get older. You have a great deal of endurance, and can resist disease well. If you are a typical Capricornian, you have good instincts for self-survival, and are practical enough to live wisely and to take care of yourself.

The Capricornian physique tends to be slim, in fact, even rather thin, with prominent bony structure. The men of this sign have what is called "craggy" faces. The women are among the most beautiful of the Zodiac, with large, expressive eyes, and a beautiful facial structure which retains its purity of outline for many, many years. Loretta Young and Marlene Dietrich are examples of the Capricornian beauty.

In general, natives of this tenth-sign are not cheerful and optimistic people. They have, in fact, a tendency toward depression. They are real worry-warts, and can literally torment themselves about matters that are so minor as to go unnoticed in the lives of other people. This outlook, of course, is damaging to the health. Fear and uncertainty are, in the last analysis, deadlier than germs. Learn to control this leaning in yourself. Fill your life with healthy activity, including outdoor exercise. Cultivate friends, and concentrate on a hobby. Learn to leave your business troubles in the office, and try to get along better with your friends and family by expecting less of them, and less of yourself. If you can train yourself to be more easy-going, and less demanding, you can improve your general health, and make your life happier, as well.

Aquarius (Jan. 21-Feb. 19): Statistics have proved that you Aquarians are among the longest-lived people in the Zodiac. Chances are that you will live nearly four years longer than will a native of one of the summer signs. Perhaps this is because the qualities of your personality are the ones that make for longevity.

In the old fable, an oak tree and a stalk of wheat were exposed to the ravages of a severe windstorm. The oak tree, standing firm and unflexible, was split by the elements, but the stalk of wheat bent to the wind, and avoided injury. As a native of Aquarius, you may be compared to the wheat. You know instinctively how to adjust to your surroundings. You do not buck the unchangeable; you do not let your emotions influence your health. You have the wisdom to accept the ups and downs of life, and so you do not break under pressure. Franklin Delano Roosevelt expressed the true Aquarian attitude when he was stricken with polio. He learned to live with his handicap—one that would have ruined the life of a lesser person.

The classic Aquarian type is slender, gracefully built, and has compelling, magnetic eyes. The general coloring is fair, with blue or gray eyes, and fine, straight hair. There is strength and dignity in the bearing of these natives. The women are often very lovely. Actress Joanne Woodward has the beauty that is associated with this sign.

Aquarians are adept at sports. Fishing, hunting, in fact any activity that gets you out into the fresh air, will be beneficial. Many of you enjoy the very active sports, such as swimming, tennis, skiing. By all means, schedule time for these pursuits. The exercise is good for your blood circulation, and will keep you from becoming sluggish. By the way, smoking is not good for you natives of Aquarius. You have probably noticed that you feel considerably better when you avoid this habit.

Pisces (*Feb*. 20-*March* 21): Chances are, if you are a typical Piscean, you have a somewhat deceptive air of fragility about you. The true Piscean, with his large, heavy-lidded eyes, his pale complexion, and fine-boned frame, gives off an aura of delicate health, in spite of the fact that his constitution is probably stronger than that of many of his sturdy-looking brothers!

Of course, in common with all other signs, Pisces inflicts its weak points. As a native of this sign, you may have trouble with your feet. Weak ankles, low arches, and metatarsal injuries are Piscean in origin. You have probably noticed, by the way, that you tend to catch cold when your feet are wet!

Astrology lays blame on Pisces for most eye disorders, too.

Have your eyes checked frequently, and take care not to strain them. Many natives of your sign are very sensitive to strong sunlight, and feel more comfortable when they wear sunglasses on bright days.

In general, Pisceans are attracted to physical stimulation. They find that their natural metabolisms are rather slow, and that liquor, caffeine, "pep pills" bring them up to a higher level of well-being. Of course, this effect of artificial stimulants is only temporary, and in the end, results in many ill-effects. Resist the urge to indulge in excesses; you, more than the natives of other signs, can be severely damaged by unwise living.

Pisceans are the most suggestible people in the Zodiac. They are easily convinced, and can even hypnotize themselves. If you, as a native of this sign, can utilize this power to serve you, you can aid yourself in your goals of health and happiness. Learn to think positively, rather than negatively. Let your imagination be your servant, rather than your master. If you can do this, you will have an excellent chance of leading a long and healthy life.

VII. Choose Your Career

"TINKER, Tailor, Soldier, Sailor" goes the children's counting rhyme. From the time we are tots, we know that among the most important decisions we will ever make, the choice of a career ranks high.

At one time—in fact, until the beginning of this century—the choice of a vocation was one that only the men of our society had to make. However, today, according to the United States Department of Labor, one out of every three workers is a woman. About 23 million women work in offices, professional and technical fields, industry, education, and the service fields. Without a doubt, women as well as men, must give serious thought to this business of making a living.

For a man, the reasons for training and studying toward a career, are obvious. He will be the "breadwinner," the head of the family. It will be his income upon which the family mainly relies. He will be spending the major part of his waking hours at his job—and for a period of some forty-five years!

But for a woman, too, work outside the home is a likelihood. Why do women work? Mostly, for the same reason men do. Practically all single women support themselves, and sometimes other members of the family, as well. Married women have gone back to work in ever increasing numbers, in order to contribute to the family income—to raise the standard of living, or to send children to college. Older women, too, now comprise a large segment of the work force. Women from 35 to 64 years of age made up 59 per cent of all women workers in 1959. And, the future holds more of the same. An expected 25 per cent increase in women workers is expected in the next decade!

When it comes to the types of occupations, women, who were at one time restricted to clerical and sales work, are now branching out into what was thought of as man's domain. We have, of course, 6½ million women clerical workers, and 1½ million saleswomen in this country, but we also have women entering such fields as law, medicine, engineering, the ministry, architecture, and so on.

With these figures showing clearly the role women now play, and will continue to play, in the productivity of our nation's industry, it is apparent that members of both sexes must be prepared to take their places in the business world. Work we must, so it well behooves us to put thought and care into career choices.

In a complex industrial society like ours, many people are trapped in work that is wrong for them. The expression, "A square peg in a round hole" is one that applies widely, unfortunately. However, no one needs to be a misfit. There is a right job for everyone! No matter what your interests, your abilities, your capacities, there is work in which you can not only find financial rewards, but also pleasure in the task, and the supreme satisfaction of fulfilling your goals.

The first step is to uncover your basic talents. Are you methodical, neat, orderly? Can you enjoy routine work? Do you have the ability to sell? Do you have an artistic gift: can you write, draw, sing, for instance? Are you dextrous? Can you teach —do you have the ability to communicate your ideas?

Secondly, what are you seeking in your work? Do you prefer to be with people, or are you happier working alone? Do you enjoy physical activity, or are you inclined toward a sedentary life? Does indoor work make you feel restricted and tied down? Can you take the rigors of outdoor work? Could you be happy working on a commission basis, or must you have a steady paycheck? Would you prefer to work for yourself, or for an established firm?

In the area of your career, as in other phases of your life, knowing what you are, and what you want, constitutes half the battle. By knowing your own self, you will gain insight into whether or not you will be happy in a given field.

Astrology provides many clues in the choice of profession. The following paragraphs will offer suggestions for the selection of a life's work, and hints about your work habits and attitudes.

Aries: (*March* 22-*Apr.* 20): Like the ram, which symbolizes your sign, you enjoy the sensation of battering down walls, seeking new expressions for your talents and enthusiasms. Yours is the realm of the pioneer. You are at your best when challenged, and like nothing more than taking on a job that is too new, too incomprehensible, or too hard for anyone else. "The difficult can be done at once," you say blithely. "The impossible takes a little longer." Not for you the tame professions, the tried and true methods. If you cannot find work in which you can utilize your individuality, your imagination, and your inventiveness, you are wasting your talents.

Wilbur Wright, the inventor of the airplane, was an Aries native. How like a member of this zodiacal division to plan and execute a design that ushered in a new age! Nearly all of the original movie stars were Ariens, or had strong Aries influence in their charts—Mary Pickford, Charlie Chaplin, Wallace Beery, Gloria Swanson—to name but a few.

Not all of us are geniuses, of course. But it should be encouraging to you to know that you are the zodiacal brother or sister of so many outstanding people, and that you, too, possess the qualities of personality that can lead you to the top in your field.

As an Arien, you approach any new task with enthusiasm, and as long as your interest is sustained, you are successful. You are happiest in work that permits you to be in a position of authority. You are pleasant to work for, because you are aware of your employees' need for approval. You do not hesitate to praise a job well done, but you are equally vocal when you are disappointed. A natural leader, you can usually get the best from your help.

There are many fields in which you can excel. The military profession is ruled by Mars, your planet, and is favorable for you. So are other Martian endeavors such as surgery and dentistry. Law enforcement is another good choice. Thomas Dewey, a native of your sign, first achieved prominence as a "racket buster" when he was District Attorney of New York.

Aries is an intellectual sign. Academic work, so long as it gives you the chance for original theories, is a sound choice. Many of you are gifted writers and speakers, particularly those of you born during the last half of the sign. Journalism is a good career. Advertising, public relations, radio and television, all present opportunities for your talents.

In selecting a career, remember that most of you Ariens are not suited to routine work. You hate monotony. When you are bored, you are unable to accomplish anything, for you become sloppy and careless. You are not happy being part of a team, either. You must work alone, or be the head of an enterprise. A major drawback is that you are an excellent starter, but dislike finishing tasks, particularly once the difficult part is done. You would rather leave this to others. You require a great deal of self-discipline to complete your work.

If you can curb your impatience, and learn to stick with a job until it is done well, you can rise to the top in your career.

Taurus (Apr. 21-May 21): You are a thoroughly practical soul. Knowing that you have two needs in your work—the need to express yourself creatively, and the need to succeed materially, you go straight about finding a career in which both are satisfied. And once you find your occupation, you rarely change. You have the ability to follow through, to stick a task out until it is completed successfully.

Taurus' star is Venus, the ruler of art and beauty. Music, in particular, is under Venusian influence. Small wonder that so many of the outstanding musicians of our time are natives of this sign. Among them are: Bing Crosby, Roberta Peters, Kate

Smith, Perry Como, Al Jolson, Rosemary Clooney, Duke Ellington, Ella Fitzgerald, Dennis Day, Benny Goodman, Patrice Munsel.

Taureans have made their mark in the entertainment field as actors too, and most of them have been known for the quiet, reserved, homey charm that the sign bestows. The late Gary Cooper, James Stewart, and Henry Fonda, all exemplify these qualities.

As a businessman, you are excellent. You are patient and methodical. You learn slowly, but you aim for, and achieve, perfection. You dislike short-cuts, and feel that if a job is worth doing, it is worth doing right. You prefer firm and reliable foundations in business. Honest and trustworthy, you are highly respected among those with whom you deal.

The world of figures is natural to you. Taureans make fine accountants, bookkeepers, bankers and financiers. Good at detail work, you seldom make any errors.

Taurus is also the sign of the farmer. You have a real ability with growing things. Livestock and poultry are also within your realm. You enjoy experimenting with raising stock, and can make a good living in this field.

In many respects, you are a really outstanding worker. However, your faults include the reluctance to try anything new. You can eventually make innovations in your work, but you have to weigh and balance first. You cannot make quick decisions. On the whole, though, you can always be counted upon to do a good job with everything you undertake. Patience and perserverance pay off, for in the end, success does come. And then, bolstered by that all-important feeling of achievement and security, you are among the happiest of people.

Gemini (May 22-June 21): Clear, quick thinking, and vibrant energy characterize your sign, Gemini. In any job in which an abstract idea has to be reduced to a formula, in which a puzzling set of circumstances has to be worked out, you shine. You have the ability to deal with an emergency, swiftly and competently. You can make instantaneous decisions, and go immediately into action.

In any field in which the worker must combine intelligence and dexterity, the Geminian is a natural choice. There is nothing you cannot do with your fingers. You excel as technicians, jewelry-makers, and in dentisty and sewing. However, you must use great caution before you enter a field which will keep you at the work-bench. You are happiest when you feel free. You are easily bored with routine, and should have a job in which there is sufficient variety to keep you interested.

Language arts are the natural forte of Geminians. Ralph Waldo Emerson, Walt Whitman, Herman Wouk, John Masefield, Thomas Mann, Jean-Paul Sartre, and Terrence Rattigan are among the many Geminians who have found success as writers and poets. It is interesting to note that Geminian President John F. Kennedy began his career as a writer, and is the winner of a Pulitzer Prize!

The Gemini wit is sparkling. Cole Porter, the lyricist whose sophisticated verse has delighted two generations, is a native of this sign. So is Bennett Cerf, the publisher who is a noted raconteur. The Duchess of Windsor, whose witty gaiety captured the heart of a King, is another Geminian. So are Beatrice Lillie, Elsa Maxwell, and that most popular comic, Bob Hope.

Geminians are natural salespeople. So articulate and persuasive are these people, that they can convince others to buy items for which they have no possible use! The man who could sell ice to an Eskimo was certainly a Gemini native! As a third-sign native, you would enjoy being a travelling salesman, or saleswoman, for you not only like to sell, but love the change of scenery travelling provides. Other good choices for you are: agent, broker, merchant.

As a Geminian, you are a loyal worker, but do not like to take advice or criticism. You work best when left to yourself. If you do not like a position, you do not hesitate to change, and so have an independent attitude in your work. In fact, you are likely to have a number of skills, and if one type of work does not pan out, can find something else.

You are inventive. You like to try new methods, and can devise ingenious aids and short-cuts. You are fussy about clean surroundings. Nothing can depress you more than a desk in a shabby, old-fashioned office.

Geminians have the ability to achieve real success, provided they fully exploit their talents, and do not allow their many interests and need for change to turn them into rolling stones.

Cancer (June 22-July 23): With your ruler, the Moon, having reign over the masses, you are apt to be successful in any endeavor in which the consumer is served. Merchandizing, particularly of articles for the home, which also comes under the dominion of your sign, is particularly favored. John Wanamaker was a Cancerian who built an empire on the basis of selling clothing and household goods. John D. Rockerfeller, the oil king, obtained his millions partly through developing a product that, again, is part of the daily life of America's millions.

Food, in particular, is a commodity with which you Cancerians have an affinity. Many of you are outstanding cooks and chefs. Still others achieve success through selling and manufacturing foodstuffs. Such industries as baking, canning, preserving, and meat slaughtering, are favorable for you.

Other aspects of the home can also present fields in which you will enjoy working. You are good as a real estate developer, home builder, real estate agent. Many Cancer women have attained fame and fortune as interior designers and decorators.

Astrology has a long arm! Somehow or other, the symbol of the home must come into your lives, Cancer. It is amusing to note that the composer of "My Old Kentucky Home," Stephen Foster, belonged to your sign!

Cancerian women are naturally motherly. They do well in any field in which children are concerned. As nursery school or primary teachers, as nurses in children's wards, for example, they are tops. They also have a reverence for old and traditional things, and can find success as antique dealers, for example.

As a native of this sign, you are an industrious worker, and can be counted upon to do a careful and accurate job. You are thrifty and prudent. You hate waste and carelessness. You enjoy leadership, and can do well as an employer or foreman, but conversely, you are a quiet, and well-liked employee. If you are treated with the courtesy and kindness you require, you are loyal and tenacious.

Many Cancerians are creative. Richard Rodgers, the song writer, Alec Templeton, the pianist, and actor Lionel Barrymore, were born under this sign. Beauty is very important to you, and you have the gift of beautifying anything with which you come in contact. The desk with the rose on it belongs to the Cancer secretary, for certain.

In choosing an occupation, you, more than the natives of many other signs, must make sure that not only your desire for success, but your inner goals as well, are satisfied. You can crumble if you are forced into a profession you dislike. At all costs, make certain that you enjoy your work for its own sake. Once you do that, you can make a name for yourself in your chosen field.

Leo (July 24-Aug. 23): Like the Lion, King of the Jungle, symbol of your sign, you are meant to be the master of all you survey. Leadership is your outstanding characteristic. You were born to rule, to dominate. Yours is the sign under which Napoleon, Julius Caesar, Alexander of Macedonia, Mussolini, and Fidel Castro were born.

You require a job in which you are not only the "boss," but in which you have an opportunity to display to the world your achievements. You cannot be content working behind the scenes. You must not be only admired, but loved, as well. With this as your goal, you are willing to work hard, even to the point of straining to the limit of your capacities. You can go on and on while others falter and drop by the sidelines.

Leo rules the theatre, and it is amazing how many of you fifth-sign natives choose that field of endeavor. Among those born under the benificent influence of your planet, the Sun, are: Lucille Ball, Billie Burke, Rory Calhoun, Eddie Fisher, Norma Shearer, Robert Taylor, Ethel Barrymore, Alfred Lunt, Mae West, and many, many other well known theatrical personalities.

It is interesting to note that even when you do not wind up in the theatre itself, you are likely to be in some field in which drama plays a part. For you, "all the world's a stage." You manage to imbue everything you do with showmanship. Leo women who are housewives, for instance, use their creative skills to decorate their homes in a dramatic manner, to prepare meals that are unusual and exotic. Those of you who choose advertising, or selling, as professions, will bring to your work original ideas, and somewhat sensational ones, at that. Publicity, or public relations are good fields for you, too. You really understand the concept of sales promotion, and know that you must "sell the sizzle, not the steak!"

Natives of your sign are successful in business, provided, again, that they have the opportunity to utilize their leadership ability. You are natural executives. You give orders well, in the manner of one who is accustomed to being understood and obeyed. You give frank and honest criticism, which is generally well-taken, for you are respected by your co-workers and employees.

In any position, you have your eye on the top rung of the ladder. A job that offers only pleasant working conditions, security, and easy hours, has no appeal for you. If there is not the chance to advance, you will not take the job.

Leo natives are naturally suited to any work that entails meeting people and being in the public eye. Receptionist for a large organization, work in a travel bureau, or ticket office at a train or airline terminal, for example, provides you with opportunities to demonstrate your charm and sparkling personality.

A danger with you fifth-sign natives is that your need to be noticed is so strong that in any work in which you do not feel appreciated enough, you are likely to sulk and lose interest. Try to develop a greater independence in regard to public approbation. After all, it is more important to meet your own high standards, than it is to have the world acclaim you, isn't it?

Virgo (Aug. 24-Sept. 23): A perfect eye for detail, and a strong analytical ability characterize the members of your sign. Versatile and adaptable, you can succeed at nearly anything you do. You are clear-thinking, intelligent, reliable, and precise. You dislike sloppy work, and have no patience with a job half done. You are a perfectionist, in every sense of the word.

Virgo has as its ruler, Mercury, which in turn has dominion over the written and spoken word. You share this planet with your sister sign, Gemini. However, where Geminians prefer the creative side of writing, you are naturally suited for research and editorial work, as well. Your writing, like everything else you do, is well-organized, precise, and right to the point. It is never bogged down with excess words. Among the great and gifted men of letters born under your stars were: Theodore Dreiser, Leo Tolstoy, William Saroyan, F. Scott Fitzgerald, and Sherwood Anderson. No other sign offers so great a concentration of literary geniuses.

Virgo also rules the service professions. You are well qualified in any work that concerns serving the basic needs of people. Many members of your sign are bookkeepers, accountants, teachers, doctors, nurses, pharmacists, or lawyers. You bring to this type of work your outstanding powers of concentration, of system and order. Naturally adept with figures, you rarely make mistakes. No tiny detail is ever beneath your consideration.

You are not fond of the limelight. You would rather work quietly, alone, knowing within your own heart that you are doing a good job, than be in a position where you are subject to criticism or approbation. You have a strong sense of responsibility, and work well without supervision.

You are not afraid of beginning at the bottom, and even of doing menial work. Long hours and short pay do not deter you, if you enjoy the nature of the work itself. To everything you do, you consistently give your all.

Although you work quickly, you give such thorough attention to detail that the results may not show up at once. You are inclined to worry and fret if things do not go well. You are insecure with short-cut methods. You are, in a position of authority, a very hard taskmaster. Few people work well enough to suit you, and you do not hesitate to criticize.

Yours is truly a dual nature, and you have many seemingly unrelated abilities. In fact, there is little at which you can not succeed. You can make a go of such diverse occupations as carpentry, farming, restaurant work, or anything that concerns food. You have a scientific, accurate mind, and at the same time, good manual dexterity.

Your best bet in choosing a vocation is to select one in which you have an opportunity to utilize your critical and analytic skills, and one in which you feel that you are of some service to others.

Libra (*Sept.* 24-*Oct.* 23) Peace and harmony are your watchwords, Libra. This is why so many of you are clergymen, diplomats, United Nations workers or State Department employees. Among those Librans whose goals have been the unity of man were Confucius, and Mahatma Gandhi, both of whom were advocates of a life in harmony with nature, and with mankind. Present day leaders include General Dwight D. Eisenhower, David Ben-Gurion, and Eleanor Roosevelt.

Beauty plays an important role in your life. Many fine artists and writers were born under Venus' rays, including Thomas Wolfe, Pablo Picasso, and Eugene O'Neill.

Among the occupations that are ascribed to your sign are jobs connected with interior decoration, jewelry, furs, clothing design, millinery, set designing, flowers and plants, and others in which a feeling for beauty is necessary.

The scales of justice symbolize your sign. Law is one of your natural professions; many of you are lawyers, judges, legal stenographers, or in other work connected with legislation and law enforcement.

Libra rules over partnerships. You are at your best in such an arrangement. You can get along with nearly anyone. You can present your ideas to co-workers and partners in such a tactful way that they are nearly always accepted and acted upon. Your sweet personality smoothes the friction that may occur whenever people disagree. You are sociable, charming, popular with those with whom your work brings you into contact. Many of you go into business with your spouses, and while this arrangement is generally fraught with problems, in your case, it works out well!

You are strongly influenced by your surroundings, and cannot work well in a rough, dirty, sordid atmosphere. You choose your own friends carefully, and are very conscious of your co-workers. You are unhappy when your work causes you to associate with people whom you would not enjoy as companions. It is wise for you to avoid such situations, if possible.

Sales work offers many opportunities to you Librans. You have great powers of persuasion. Your charm carries you through. By the way, modeling is a good career for you lovely Libra ladies.

If you select work in which there is no opportunity to vent your artistic talents, try to make up for it by having a creative hobby. You will find that if you have an outlet, you will be a happier person, and so will have more to offer in your day-to-day work.

Scorpio (Oct. 24-Nov. 22): Of all the signs of the Zodiac, yours is the one in which there is the most diversity. Natives of Scorpio are so different from each other that it is difficult to draw a general pattern, particularly about their vocational abilities. However, it may be said the quality you have in common is that you enjoy work that is difficult, that is a challenge, and that offers you an opportunity to put into use your excellent powers of investigation. You enjoy ferreting out the motives of others, and you also enjoy work in which you have to "second guess" someone.

Among those natives of your sign who have put the Scorpio abilities to work are explorer Richard E. Byrd. He illustrates the exceptional courage endowed by this sign. Another pioneer in the field of exploration—this time of the mind and emotions—is George Gallup, who founded "Gallup Polls." Here again, we have the Scorpio desire to penetrate a frontier. Many foremost detectives and mystery writers are born under your star.

Excellence in the field of exploration and investigation can also lead you into such careers as laboratory technician, chemist, physicist, pathologist, physician, psychiatrist, surgeon.

Scorpions are athletic, and enjoy feats of physical prowess. Many fine athletes, among them baseball's great Ted Williams, belong to this sign.

In any work you choose, you work hard. You are very thorough, turning out perfected work, and always promptly. You aim for the top in any endeavor; success is one of your guiding lights. You not only have great ability, you are the very opposite of lazy. You will work out new and better methods, and concentrate on upping your work output.

You have good intellectual abilities, and can quickly discern the main point in any theory. You learn easily, memorize well. In scholarship, you will plug ahead, making certain, again, that you have been as thorough in your approach as possible.

Scorpions have great powers of concentration, and this combined with their innate abilities, usually makes them successful in their chosen fields. Not only, in fact, are they intelligent, there is frequently a streak of genius in their make-up. If it is true, as has been said, that genius is 10 per cent inspiration, and 90 per cent perspiration, it is easy to see why there are so many Scorpio natives in the roster of the Hall of Fame!

Sagittarius (Nov. 23-Dec. 22): Yours is a philosophic nature, Sagittarius, and one that is characterized by good judgment, intelligence, and balance. You are in pursuit of knowledge at all times—life is a quest of wisdom for you. For this reason, you have a depth that is not found in natives of some other signs.

The sign of the Archer has produced many of the world's great thinkers. Among them are: Spinoza, the philosopher; Emily Dickinson, the poet; and Gustave Flaubert, the writer. Each of these people is important not only for the beauty of his writing, but for his or her penetrating understanding of the nature of man and of the universe.

Sagittarius is a sign of accomplishment. Among other natives who have attained fame and fortune, as well as the admiration of their fellow-man are: Andrew Carnegie, the tycoon; writers Thomas Carlyle, Willa Cather, Kenneth Roberts; statesman Benjamin Disraeli.

Wit plays a large part in your life. Natives of your sign have perhaps the best sense of humor in the Zodiac. This is exemplified by the contributions of such famous humorists as: Mark Twain, James Thurber, and Noel Coward.

Your personality is a great asset to you, and many people who have made names for themselves primarily on the basis of their appeal to others are Sagittarians. This list includes: Frank Sinatra, Mary Martin, and Betty Grable.

Any field in which animals are concerned is natural for you. You would do well as a veterinarian, animal breeder, rancher. An interesting sidelight: none other than Walt Disney, the man who rode a mouse to fame and fortune, is a Sagittarian!

In your work, you enjoy acclaim. You do not want to have your achievements hidden. You enjoy governmental work, for example, and many of you become clergymen and lecturers. You are at your best when you are in the public eye.

Sagittarians have good work habits. They are competent and swift. They enjoy progressive ideas, and like challenges. Most important to them is that they have a feeling of freedom, and a job in which they do not have to account for their time is preferred.

As a Sagittarian, you enjoy travel, preferably to foreign lands. Training in foreign languages is rarely lost on a Sagittarian youngster, for the chances are very good that at some time in his life he will be able to use them. In fact, many of you settle in lands far from your birth. You quickly learn the mores of the new locale, and are immediately at home. Any work in which long distance travel plays a part is favored for you.

As an executive, you have many talents. You are good-humored and pleasant to be with. You make those who work for you feel appreciated and confident. Your enthusiasm for a task is contagious. You are an efficient and popular boss.

With your high intellect, your bounding energy and good

health, your pleasing personality and many talents, you should be able to succeed in nearly anything to which you turn your hand.

Capricorn (Dec. 23-Jan. 20): Natives of your sign have been called the "work horses" of the Zodiac. You are characterized by your outstanding ability for hard labor, and your will to succeed.

Conservative in everything you do, you find the opinion of others important to you. You are fearful of going out on a limb and making a fool of yourself. You like established professions, and you like to enjoy a good reputation. In your dealings with the public you demonstrate this keen awareness of your status in the eyes of the world. Such Capricornian statesmen as Chancellor Konrad Adenauer of Germany; France's Pierre Mendes-France; and former Vice President Richard Nixon, exhibited this conventional approach.

You are thorough in everything you do. Once you set out to accomplish a goal, you do not stop until you have utilized every bit of your ability and talent. That is why so many Capricornians not only achieve prominence, but greatness, as well. Capricorn native Pablo Casals is considered in musical circles to be the greatest musician alive today. Louis Pasteur, the scientist, exhibited the dogged persistence endowed by his sign, in his work. Isaac Newton, the great mathematician, Benjamin Franklin and Alexander Hamilton, were other accomplished Capricornians.

Capricorn has an affinity not only for success, but for material acquisition. Many men and women who became millionaires were born under this sign, including industrial giant Pierre S. Du Pont, and Helena Rubinstein, who is said to be the world's most successful businesswoman.

You are businesslike. You have no patience with any business method that is not sound. You like to arrange and revamp systems, until the organization runs on greased wheels. For this reason, you star in fields concerning the manufacturing and producing of goods. You also are good in merchandising.

Neat and orderly, you are careful craftsmen. You can succeed as a builder, an architect, or a technician. Many of you make excellent engineers, particularly in the mechanical and electrical fields.

Most Capricornians are good at figures, and enjoy all phases of financial work. Among the professions Capricorn natives have made good in are accountancy, banking, bookkeeping, and statistical work. You are accurate researchers, too.

As a Capricornian, you do not believe that luck plays much part in success. Instead, you chalk up the attainment of your goals to hard work. You have no objection to starting at the bottom, provided you feel that yours is not a dead-end profession, and that you will make good sooner or later. You are not easily bored; through strength of will and determination you can continue long after others will have abandoned a goal as not being attainable.

Sometimes it is difficult for you to get along with your co-workers, for you tend to be somewhat intolerant. You are suited to a position in which you work alone; and although you may complain about being lonely, you can get more accomplished, and will get a greater feeling of satisfaction from being on your own.

There is little of the "jack of all trades" in your disposition. You are not likely to change jobs frequently, but rather you work steadfastly in one profession, until you make a name for yourself. Success is of vital importance to you. There is no one more content than a Capricornian who has achieved his goals, nor more miserable than one who feels he failed. No other satisfactions can compensate you for the one you most seek in life—success.

Aquarius (Jan. 21-Feb. 19): It is a fact that there is an overwhelmingly large percentage of genius among the natives of your sign. Dr. Ellsworth Huntington, of Yale, in his book, "Season of Birth," has proved that more famous people were born at this time than during any other season of the year. It is said that 80% of the people in the Hall of Fame claim your sign as theirs! With this as your heritage, how can you fail?

There is literally nothing an Aquarian cannot do if he sets his mind to it. You are endowed with so great an intelligence and understanding of humanity, that greatness is within your reach.

Aquarians have made names for themselves in every field of endeavor. Many prominent American leaders were born under this sign, including Abraham Lincoln, Franklin Roosevelt, General Douglas MacArthur, and Adlai Stevenson. Each of these men signifies an important aspect of the Aquarius personality! Franklin Roosevelt's concept of government was radically different from those of his predecessors. He demonstrated the Aquarian ability to dissolve old conditions and create new ones. Abraham Lincoln is a foremost example of Aquarius' great tolerance and feeling for humanity. General Douglas MacArthur is, of course, a truly magnetic person, who can inspire not only confidence, but even, for large numbers of people, adoration. Adlai Stevenson is known for his great charm, which is universal in appeal, as proved by the favorable press he has received in all the countries of the world. Incidentally, no better spot could be found for a native of this sign than in the United Nations, the congress of world powers, and the institution that serves the greatest numbers of peoples of the world. The U.N. itself is Aquarian in its concept.

Aquarians are inventive—more so than any other sign except possibly Gemini. In this area natives of Aquarius are in the forefront, for they have more stick-to-itiveness than do their Geminian brothers. Thomas Edison was a native of this sign.

Nearly all Aquarians have fine taste, and many of them have definite artistic ability, as well. Among the great names in the arts who were eleventh-sign natives, were poets Robert Burns, Lord Byron; writers Lewis Carroll (author of Alice in Wonderland); Somerset Maugham, Edgar Allan Poe, John O'Hara, Charles Dickens, James Joyce, Sinclair Lewis; composer Wolfgang Mozart; violinist Mischa Elman; pianist Artur Rubinstein; conductor Walter Damrosch; guitarist Andres Segovia.

The Aquarian personality is magnetic. No one illustrated the power of this magnetism better than the late Clark Gable, who enthralled two generations of women with his masculine charm. Other theatrical personalities who demonstrate the Aquarius appeal are: Tallulah Bankhead, Randolph Scott, Eddie Cantor, Lana Turner, John Barrymore, Jack Benny and Katherine Cornell.

It is possible to list page after page of important Aquarians, but by now the message should be clear to you. Yours is a sign of achievement, and it is up to you to make of yourself what you wish.

As an Aquarian, you should avoid routine work. You work best on your own, and often rather spasmodically. You cannot bear to have a boss "breathing down your neck." You can handle responsibility perfectly, but hate to take orders.

You are best suited to some sort of work in which humanity at large is benefited. You are happy in politics, social work, governmental positions. The law may hold your interest, or you may find a slot in academic work. Being a teacher, preferably in the higher grades, (for you would rather work on an adult level), is suitable to your talents. Likewise you do well in any position in which yours is a public trust, such as insurance, stocks and bonds, or other field in which your honesty and the feeling of confidence you inspire comes to the forefront.

Among all this array of talents, there is only one danger for which you must watch. Beware of letting your daydreams take the place of achievement. You have a tendency to procrastinate. Remember, you must take your opportunities as they appear, and not wait for imaginary ones. Make the most of the present, and the future will take care of itself.

Pisces (Feb. 20-March 21): Your sign is characterized by two fish, each swimming in an opposite direction. In a sense this is symbolic of your vocational abilities, as it is of your personality in general. On the one hand, there is the practical side of your nature—the one that has to do with the achievement of set goals, the hard work to carry them out, the painstaking attention to detail. The other symbolizes the mystical side of your nature, your tremendous imagination, your artistic abilities.

Art plays a large part in your life even if you are not engaged in it for a living. Many great artists were born under your sign, including Renaissance sculptor and painter Michelangelo; composer Frederic Chopin; poet Henry Wadsworth Longfellow. The sign rules dancing—lovely Cyd Charisse carries out Pisces potential in this field.

Your imagination may well be the fountainhead of your success. Professions in which many of you can succeed include anything connected with the theatre—acting, writing, set or costume designing, lighting. Color is important to you, and anything in which you can make use of your fine taste is a vocational possibility. You might think about ceramics, interior decoration, industrial designing.

One cannot think of the great men and women born under the sign of Pisces without mentioning Albert Einstein. He, too, exemplifies another Piscean aptitude—an ear for the "music of the spheres." Natives of your sign are ruled by the mystical Neptune, and have a remarkable understanding of the nature of all life. They are intuitive, and can respond to forces that are neither seen nor heard by their more plebeian brothers and sisters.

Now for the "other fish"—the side of you that is pragmatic, detail-minded, businesslike. Natives of your sign are good in the service industries or in anything that concerns the health and welfare of people. The restaurant business, or anything concerned with the preparation and merchandising of food, is a good choice. It is interesting, by the way, that the proprietors of three of the best known American restaurants—Mike Romanoff, of Hollywood's fine restaurant, Sherman Billingsley of the Stork Club, and Mac Kriendler, of New York's famous 21 Club, are all natives of Pisces.

Your sign rules institutions, and many of you are engaged in work that helps the needy and sick. Nursing, teaching, social welfare work, psychiatry and medicine, are possible choices for you. You have great sympathy for those in distress, and can not only care for them physically but help them spiritually, as well.

You are among the most adaptable of all people. You can take on the coloration of your surroundings and adjust to conditions that other people would find disturbing. However, because you are so sensitive, it is important for you to find work in which you do not come under sordid influences. It is better for you to seek a new line of work than to be in surroundings which are not uplifting.

You possess a good deal of determination, and are intelligent, loyal and dedicated. You are methodical and neat. You get on well with employers, employees, and co-workers, because of your gentle charm.

Pisces natives are the dreamers of the world. If you can back up this visionary outlook with hard work and determination, there is no limit to what you can achieve.

VIII. The House You Live In

AMERICANS are home-minded. Since the end of World War II, more and more of us own our own homes. With an easing of credit restrictions, the availability of long-term mortgages, and most of all, a higher standard of living, the dream of owning your own home has become a reality.

Have you ever stopped to consider just how much you are worth financially? Chances are, you will begin by estimating the value of your house. For the average family, this purchase represents the largest single outlay of cash, and involves the greatest amount of credit buying. The ownership of a home usually represents the bulk of a family's life savings.

However, this is only part of the reason that buying a house is one of the most important decisions a family has to face. Not only is the right choice important for financial reasons, there are less tangible, and perhaps even more meaningful ones. The town or city in which you live, the street, the school district, your neighbors, all shape your life and the lives of your children. The actual structure of the house itself prescribes your family life. Is there a backyard for the family to play in, or room for indoor recreation? Is the kitchen large enough for the family to congregate, or is there space for formal entertaining? Is there enough room for the younger generation to have privacy for themselves and their friends? All these considerations are important, for a family has to modify its activities in terms of space.

We would be lucky indeed if we could all choose our favorite locations in which to live, but this is something that is rarely possible. However, if you are fortunate enough to be able to just pick a spot on the map, consider first the climate in which you are most comfortable. Secondly, the living costs of the area must be kept in mind. Generally speaking, a dollar goes farther in the South and Midwest than it does on either coast. The farther from an industrial area and major city, the cheaper the cost of living. Building costs in the suburbs of the larger cities, New York, Chicago, etc., may be as much as 25% higher than in the rest of the country.

Secondly, in buying a house, you must know what sort of a dwelling you can afford. A good rule of thumb, one that is used by mortgage agencies, is to figure a family can afford a house costing up to two and one half times their annual income. Another rule is that the yearly running expenses, including mortgage payments, taxes, heat, repair and maintenance should not exceed 25% of the annual income.

Now for the house itself. Whether you buy a new or old dwelling, or build one yourself, you will want to have the smallest repair and upkeep bill possible. It is always wise to consult an expert who can advise you about the roof, foundation, wiring, plumbing and heating systems. For example, an older house is usually roomier than a new one at the same price, but you must consider, among other things, whether its wiring will accommodate today's appliances—the washing machine, dryer, air conditioner, and so on, or whether you may have to spend as much as $500 or more to rewire. It is usually a good investment to have a specialist go over the house before you make the down payment.

The neighborhood, too, must be considered. Does your family desire privacy or social activity? If there are school age children in the family, you must be sure that the school is convenient. Spend some time investigating before you buy. Find out where shopping centers, churches, and other facilities are.

Astrology can help you to make the best choice in buying a house in which you and your family can live happily. The sort of person you are determines your needs in a home. Your manner of living, family relationships, tastes and likes must be taken into consideration in this most important purchase. By knowing yourself, and understanding your mode of living, you can make a wise selection.

Aries (March 22-April 20): As an Arien, you need to establish your own home. In spite of your adventurous, roving nature, you have a strong desire for a home base to which you can retire from the fray of your active life. You have a deep sense of self; and whatever else it may be, your home will be uniquely and individually yours.

For most Ariens, a house in a large city is preferred. You like to be near excitement and hustle-bustle. However, should you make your home in the suburbs, try to be near city conveniences, for you have little patience with tedious commuting. As you like the changing seasons, the East or Northeast is a good choice; however, you may also be tempted to warmer climates, for you enjoy outdoor sports.

A good choice of design for you first-sign natives would be a ranch house. You like a level plot, a home built as low and rambling as possible. Your preference is for informal architecture. A stone and clapboard house might be a good choice, rather than brick. You are happiest in a casual setting, so avoid too-careful landscaping. By all means, try to have your walls plastered so that you can vary your color scheme, changing from one vivid, gay shade to another when the mood strikes you. Aries women are quick and efficient housekeepers; so an ultra-modern kitchen, full of labor-saving devices, is a better choice than other luxury expenditures.

Aries people are easy to "sell." In fact, a danger is that you may be inclined to make a hasty decision regarding your home. Another Aries problem is extravagance. You don't mean to get in over your head; but in the flush of acquiring something you really want, you may vastly overestimate your ability to pay. Make sure of your down payment—and even more certain you can manage the upkeep of the house you select.

Taurus (Apr. 21-May 21): "Land, lots of lovely land" and a house built like a fortress is your choice, Taurus. You will check to be sure your dwelling has a slate roof, copper gutters, brass plumbing and the driest cellar in town! Quality is your foremost consideration.

When planning that dream house, remember that you desire peace, quiet and harmony. Select a location in the country or in one of the quieter suburbs. Be sure that your dwelling stands back from the road and is surrounded by acreage on all sides. Though your abode will be sturdy, it will be modest rather than ostentatious; and your extra funds may well go into the landscaping. It is in gardening that you really shine.

Your home does not have to be new, for you like to repair and remodel. With Venusian love of beauty, you will choose warm, serene colors and gleaming woods. You prefer hardwood floors to the newer surfaces; and you will give careful attention to hardware, tile and other details.

Taurus people have a horror of debt and are likely to be very careful before making a down payment. You will be sure to carry as small a mortgage as possible. However, since the Taurean is generally a good provider, ready cash is usually no problem.

Gemini (May 22-*June* 21): You Gemini natives are restless and easily bored. Your need for variety and the duality of your nature may prompt you to own not one but several different homes during the course of your life. By the time you buy and furnish one house, you may be thinking about a change!

As a soothing, restful atmosphere helps you to feel and work at your best, try to select a site in the suburbs or in the country, where it is quiet. You consider flat ground uninteresting; a hilly location would be good for you.

Imaginative and resourceful, the Gemini buyer is often able to capture a bargain in a house, for he sees possibilities that may escape his less mercurial brothers. Many a dwelling, bypassed as hopeless by other shoppers, has been transformed into a thing of beauty by a clever Gemini purchaser. Since you are also ingenious and handy, you may be able to save labor costs by remodeling and rebuilding.

Gemini natives like to do things a little differently from anyone else. Space and labor-saving gadgets are usually found in their homes. An absolute necessity for a Gemini woman is a good deal of wall space in her living room, for she likes to rearrange her furniture frequently. Another necessity is some room of your own, where you can "escape" for a few hours.

You need to use caution in financial matters, and this applies directly to the purchase of a house. You have a tendency to purchase more things than you need. Many a thoroughly honest Geminian has been surprised to find his credit rating has slipped because he has incurred a number of debts. Remember that buying a home is usually your largest expenditure; be sure you have a clear picture of your finances first.

Cancer (June 22-July 23): You are a rare Cancerian if you do not already—or have not made plans to—own your own home. You will gladly forgo vacations and costly clothing to make a down payment on that dream house!

If possible, you should select a section of the country where the winters are not too long or cold. A good location for Cancerians is a site near a lake or stream. Choose a wooded plot, one where you will be sure to have a front and back yard. You'll certainly want room for a barbecue pit and dining patio.

A conservative style of architecture is best for you. You will avoid the stark, contemporary house. Comfort is your keynote, and you don't enjoy anything in which coziness is sacrificed for high style. A charming Cape Cod house would be a good selection.

You like antiques, quaint lighting fixtures and hardware. Since Cancer women are wonderful cooks, the kitchen is likely to be the heart of their homes. Be sure to build or buy a house with plenty of pantry space! If it can be managed, a separate dining room is a good plan, for Cancerians frequently entertain for dinner. Plenty of play space for the children is another necessity. A finished playroom in the basement is a wise idea.

Cancer natives like to buy the best and will pay a good price

THE HOUSE YOU LIVE IN

for it. However, they are not extravagant and know value. In buying a home, they often pay cash. Bankers find Cancerians excellent risks; generally, they pay off mortgages more quickly than the average person. Needless to say, their residences are always fully covered by liability and fire and theft insurance.

Leo (July 24-Aug. 23): Like the proud Lion that is symbolic of this sign, you Leo natives feel caged in small quarters. You need a large house, with spacious grounds. A home to be proud of is your desire, for you like to look both prosperous and glamourous.

You Leo people are not restricted to one area or section of the country. Any place will do, as long as it is near mountains, rivers and forests. Hale and hearty, you enjoy almost any climate.

The best type of house for you would be a stately Georgian Colonial or an imposing English home. You prefer brick and stone to other building materials. You'll select a house set back from the street, as it is more impressive.

Like all fire-sign people, you enjoy vivid color. Gold is a good choice for the interior of your dwelling. Your living room should have a fireplace or large window or some other dramatic focal point. Generally, Leo women dislike housework; and although they enjoy everything in their homes that is luxurious, a large, beautiful kitchen is not as important as other features in a house. By the way, it is interesting to notice how many Leo natives use some form of monogram as part of the interior or exterior decoration of their abodes.

As with most fire-sign natives, extravagance may be your problem. You do not like to resist a purchase when it appears you cannot afford it. Make certain, before you buy or build, that you will not need to deny yourself other comforts in order to pay the mortgage.

Virgo (Aug. 24-Sept. 23): Shrewd and practical, you Virgoans make careful selections when you shop for houses. Your home is never the one with the leaky roof or the half-finished expansion attic. In your careful, competent way, you will make sure that everything you own is in good condition.

Virgo likes solitude. If it can be arranged, a dwelling in the suburbs is preferred; but modern conveniences must always be available. You scorn anything new and flashy. An older house, one that is lived in, on a large plot surrounded by trees, would please you. Although you cherish the friends you make, you don't like to be too close to your neighbors; so your home is likely to have a fence around it.

You are among the handiest people in the Zodiac. Virgo men find it easy to pine-panel a den or install a new floor. You like old things—antique fixtures, bricks and woodwork made into novel decoration. A living room with a fireplace would be a source of pleasure to you. Virgo women are excellent house-keepers and insist on plenty of closet space. "A place for every-thing and everything in its place" is your motto. A super-efficient kitchen would make a big hit with the ladies.

You earth-sign people get good value for your money. You are careful and thrifty shoppers and may well take years before you pick a house or plot. You have a fear of overpaying and cannot enjoy a purchase if you feel you did not get your full money's worth. Once committed to a mortgage, you will system-atically and carefully pay it off. You are a fine credit risk and should have no trouble arranging for the financing of your home.

Libra (Sept. 24-Oct. 23): For you Librans, beauty and harmony count above all else. Your house may not be the largest or most imposing one on the block, but chances are it will have the most tasteful decoration.

Libra is happy in a large city, regardless of climate, living costs or conditions. If it is necessary for you to live in the country or suburbs, you will be as close to a main road as pos-sible. Your home need not be a large one, but it must have a spacious living room. You are never far from friends and love to entertain.

A split-level house would be a good choice for you, for you are conservative and modern at the same time and enjoy combining the old with the new. A house with a center hall would please your sense of proportion and balance. The land-scaping of your dwelling is not of great importance, for although you enjoy the beauty of flowers and trees, you consider gardening menial and try to avoid it. You would enjoy a picture window overlooking someone else's garden!

Libra women, even those in modest financial circumstances, have the ability to create beautiful, restful interiors. Soft colors, deep rugs, full draperies are important to you; and if need be, you will sacrifice on your house's construction to be sure you can afford fine decoration.

You Librans are scrupulously honorable; and once you undertake a debt, you are sure to make good. However, be sure you know exactly what you are contracting for when you buy your home. You like a bargain, and sometimes bargains have a way of not being all they seem to be.

Scorpio (Oct. 24-Nov. 22): You Scorpio natives are proud of your families, and your home is your castle! As you are fixed-sign natives, you dislike making changes. Conservative, thrifty, shrewd and wise, you choose your houses carefully and stay with your choice. Your homes are always individual in some way, expressive of your strong, unique personalities.

Scorpions belong to the water triplicity. You enjoy a climate that provides plenty of rain. The Pacific Northwest is ideal. If this is not possible, try to select a site in a small town near a body of water. You do not like to be close to other people and need to have a large plot of land around your dwelling.

A ranch house or one of Mediterranean style is best for you. You dislike climbing stairs, so need to have all the rooms on one floor. Your house should be on the shady side of the street. Try to have awnings or jalousies as part of its decoration; you hate the glare of sunlight.

Scorpio women are methodical and keep immaculate houses, but luxury is the keynote, rather than efficiency. A super-modern kitchen is less important than a lovely patio under the trees. Incidentally, every appliance in a Scorpio household has a guarantee or warranty, which is carefully filed away.

You cannot be sold anything you are not sure of, and this is especially true when you are house hunting. You know just what you like, and are suspicious of real estate brokers' claims unless you can see for yourself. Once you make up your mind to buy, you will, even though it may cost more than you had planned, for you don't deny yourself anything you really want.

Sagittarius (Nov. 23-Dec. 22): A house that lets the outdoors in is your desire, Sagittarius. You like freedom, air, plenty of space. Your home will be situated so that it is open to the sun and wind during all seasons of the year.

You ninth-sign natives dislike thickly settled communities. You like to be a distance from your next-door neighbor. A community which provides plenty of recreational facilities would satisfy you—particularly one in which there are riding ranges and woods in which you can take the family hiking.

A ranch house would be satisfactory to a Sagittarian. These progressive, far-sighted people like up-to-date things and usually prefer to build or to buy new houses, rather than remodel old ones. You are rather gadget-happy, and one may be sure to find the latest conveniences in your kitchen. The women are good managers and good planners. Their homes are usually arranged to function with a minimum of care. You enjoy decorating with such colors as red, coral, deep gold, anything in the beige family. Vinyl tile floors, plastic finishes on walls, anything that is easy to care for and lively in color is your choice.

In common with other fire signs, Sagittarius produces many people who are too easy with their money. However, there is also a certain type of Sagittarian who is thrifty to the point of being overcautious. Generally speaking, you Jupiter-ruled natives are gamblers and will take a chance on purchases that look risky. Watch your step, for buying a house is a big move. It never hurts to have an appraiser or some expert reinforce your opinion before you sign on the dotted line.

Capricorn (Dec. 23-Jan. 20): A dignified, older house, even one with an historical past, is Capricorn's desire. You conservative people cherish tradition. Your practical nature insists on careful workmanship. A hastily-built, flimsy house will never suit you, even as a temporary residence.

You enjoy the changing seasons, provided the climate is not too hot in the summer. If you can manage to live in the East, preferably New England, you will be happy. You prefer a small community, one with tradition. You don't like noise and excitement. It is necessary for you to have privacy from your neighbors.

Your house should be on the shady side of the street, set back from the road, surrounded by shrubbery. Even if you buy a new house, you will never choose anything flashy—and it will soon assume a lived-in look. You are sure to make additions to your house, for Capricorn men are very handy—and Capricorn women like everything "just so." Born workers, these gals keep sparkling homes. Your dwelling will have freshly painted shutters and shining trim at all times. You have little patience with anything that doesn't stay in good repair. You will make sure, before you hand over your down payment, that your house has good plumbing, heating and that all the appliances are ones with well-known names.

Capricorn natives are thrifty shoppers. They ask for and get guarantees on everything. Adept with figures, they can arrange for the best bank mortgage and always receive the lowest rate of interest. They seldom get into any purchase that is over their heads.

Aquarius (Jan. 21-Feb. 19): That steel and glass house, newer than a space rocket, may well belong to an Aquarian. In home building, these "new-age" people step in where angels fear to tread! Sure of their own taste, which is usually very good, they will take a chance on a style of architecture which would not attract their more conservative brothers.

You like convenience in transportation, so a home in a suburb just outside the city is a good bet. You do enjoy seclusion, yet need to be near good highways or railroad lines. High ground is your selection for a site. Given a choice, you would probably like to live in the Northwest. However, you hate to move and will settle down in one spot anywhere as soon as you can.

Your actual physical surroundings are not as important to you as they are to natives of other signs. However, you love your beautiful possessions. A home with a workshop is necessary for you, for you are devoted to your hobbies. A darkroom for the men and a sewing room for the ladies would be good features.

You dislike being cramped, and a large bedroom is always desirable. Aquarian women like to arrange "kitchen-living-rooms," for although they dislike drop-in company, they are excellent hostesses and like to be with their guests while they are preparing meals.

You Aquarians fear debt and pay cash whenever possible. In buying a house, try to arrange for a mortgage that permits you to pay it off sooner than full term, if you wish, without a penalty.

Pisces (Feb. 20-March 21): A perfect house for a Piscean will surely be comfortable and spacious. It will never be pretentious or too extreme in its design. Almost certainly, its exterior will be a pastel shade.

Like your water-sign cousins, Scorpio and Cancer, you prefer a home in a coastal city or near a lake or stream. As you appreciate the finer things of life and are very sensitive to your surroundings, you will be sure to select a home in a fine community. You are choosy about the people with whom you associate. Your neighbors will be looked over carefully before you decide upon your location.

A roomy older home, with verandas and porches, would be a good choice for you. If you select a new house, it will not be one of the ultra-modern ones. Competent housekeepers, Pisces women do not like menial work, and their homes are usually equipped with features that make for easy maintenance.

As you are gifted in imagination and artistic beauty, the decor of your home will always be beautiful. You take on the color of your environment, and a dingy house can actually make you ill. Therefore, it is very important for you to work closely with painters and carpenters to be certain you get just what you want.

Pisces natives need to exercise care in financial planning for their homes. They have a tendency to be extravagant. If they can guard against this, they can select homes that will please both the practical and artistic sides of their dual natures.

IX. Your Leisure Time

According to labor leader Walter Reuther, the four-day work week will soon be a reality! This is not as far-fetched as it sounds, for within this century, the number of hours per week that the average person works has been shortened from 72 to 40 —and in many industries, 35. Whether this is entirely good or not is debatable, but this much is true: most of us have more spare time now than ever before. Even after you deduct the hours devoted to work, sleep, going to and coming from your job, about 22% of your time is free for leisure activity.

In addition, more people are living longer and gaining a chance to enjoy the fruits of a well-earned retirement. Older folks have "time on their hands"—but not always the know-how of how to best enjoy it.

The question of how to put leisure time to constructive use, is one that puzzles many people. "We are always getting ready to live," wrote Emerson, "but never living." Here, alas, is the problem. When we do find ourselves with some spare time, often we refuse to use it for recreation. Perhaps this is a residual effect of our Puritan heritage, which taught us that "life is real, life is earnest." Nothing so frivolous as play was considered to be a necessary part of life.

Actually, nothing is further from the truth than the belief that recreation is a form of self-indulgence. The Menninger Clinic recently established, after a series of interviews and tests, that mentally healthy people had twice as many play interests as those who were emotionally disturbed. So, it seems, all work and no play make Jack not only a dull boy, but a mixed up one, too!

To start at the beginning, what should you do with your leisure time? First, of course, you must set aside time for hobbies and sports, and for vacations. Secondly, in selecting a satisfying form of recreation, look for one that will give you:

A change of pace from your daily activities. For instance, if you are an office worker, look for an active sport; if you do physical work, a quiet activity is best.

A form of recreation that engrosses you completely, and helps you to take your mind off your worries.

A way to let off excess emotion. Healthy people find it is infinitely better to wham a tennis ball, than to strike back at a cranky boss!

Happily, the field of recreation is almost unlimited. There are sports of course: softball, racket games, handball, horseshoes, shuffleboard, golf, archery, swimming, boating, horseback riding, skating, skiing, and others much too numerous to list.

Then there are hobbies, and these too, encompass a great number. Collecting, handiwork, woodworking, games such as cards, chess, and checkers. There are forms of self-expression that serve a worthwhile purpose as recreation: music, drawing, painting, dancing, writing, acting and photography.

We must not, of course, forget the spectator sports, such as baseball, ice hockey, basketball games, tennis matches, and so on. And then, of course, there are always T.V., plays, concerts, and the movies.

Daily play comes under the heading of recreation, and so, of course, do vacations. In planning for those "two weeks with pay," again, the goal is to select some change from the everyday routine. Whether you choose to travel, to stay at a resort, or to retreat to your own summer cottage, a vacation should provide rest as well as varied experiences, so that you return refreshed, relaxed, and ready to go again!

There are, of course, certain considerations to bear in mind in choosing good leisure time outlets. Your pocketbook, most likely, will set limits. The amount of time you actually have, the availability of facilities all dictate your selections, to an extent. But in the last analysis, here is a phase of your life in which you can allow your own interests and desires to take over.

The sort of person you are tells you what type of leisure time activities you will prefer. A vigorous Sagittarian, for example, will probably prefer an active form of play, while a Capricornian is drawn to a recreation that provides more than simply diversion. In the following paragraphs, you will find some suggestions. Read, picture yourself engaging in the various sports and hobbies, and if one appeals to you—try it. You might have a lot of fun!

Aries (March 22-April 20): For you, as an Arien, leisure time is a precious and rare commodity. Your life is so full that time on your hands is a most unlikely burden! If you are typical of your sign, you are interested in so many things, and have so many various projects on tap, that your problem is likely to be how to accomplish all you have contracted to do, rather than how to divert yourself.

You enjoy active vacations. Not for you, lounging in a hammock with a glass of lemonade in your hands, watching the summer day draw to a close! You may, in the frantic moments of your hurried life long for such a rest, but when the time comes to take those "two weeks with pay," you are more likely to make arrangements to travel, or to sign up at some resort in which you can find the athletic facilities you like.

Ariens have a broad streak of adventure in their make-up. They are fond of travel, particularly to new and exotic places. On a trip to Mexico, for example, you have no fear of traveling up narrow winding roads, nor of eating new and unusual foods. You can enjoy a trip to Europe, or to any foreign place, for you have the ability to take changes well, and do not become upset if you are without your accustomed creature comforts. Plumbing is less important to you than excitement! You are open-minded, make friends quickly among traveling acquaintances, and can accept the unfamiliar without losing your equilibrium.

Almost any sort of a vacation in which you have freedom of motion is inviting to you. You become easily bored with regimentation, however, and a planned tour on which every hour is accounted for, is not as thrilling to you as a vacation in which you are free to choose your activities and travel sites. If you travel, by all means take short bus tours, but think it over before you sign up for anything with a carefully planned itinerary.

As far as your daily leisure time is concerned, you are likely to be drawn into recreation in which there is companionship. A little theatre group might be fun, for you enjoy the spotlight. A discussion group, such as a book club, is also appealing. You have many opinions, and like to make them heard! Volunteer work with such organizations as Red Cross has much to offer you, and vice versa. You are suited to disaster work and can be of much aid in any emergency. You like to be at the scene of the crisis, where you can function in a cool and efficient way. Any occupation in which the military forces are involved is good for you. You have the aptitude to do volunteer civil defense work, for instance, and the men of your sign are often members of the voluntary fire department, or police force.

Sedentary hobbies do not hold much appeal for you. As a rule you Ariens do not have the patience for stamp collections, for example, and rarely will study anything long enough to become expert in the field.

Many Arien men are handy at woodworking. They are very inventive, and like to work out original ideas. Arien Thomas Jefferson, designed all his furniture, and the Aries touch is evident in such designs as chairs that unfold and become tables as well!

The women of this sign have some ability at sewing and handiwork. They have good taste, sometimes rather extreme, but always attractive. However, they may lack the patience to complete an ambitious project, in which hours of repetitious detail work is necessary.

As far as your friendships go, you find these very satisfying. You immediately become part of any group you join, and can thaw out the shyest person. You are a good and loyal friend. People enjoy having you around because you are entertaining and good company, and because they sense the sincerity of your feeling.

You are naturally good at sports, and enjoy them—usually the more dangerous the better! Swimming, skiing and hockey are good selections. You are highly competitive, and love a fast game of ball, or tennis. Aries rules firearms; many of you are expert marksmen, and enjoy hunting and fishing. Bowling is a good choice for an indoor sport. By and large you do not take to spectator sports, for you would rather participate in athletics than sit in the stands and watch.

Taurus (Apr. 21-*May* 21): Your ruler, Venus, has dominion over art and music, parties, play, and anything in which gaiety, beauty and laughter have a part. This is not to say that you, as a Taurean, are a frivolous creature. Far from it! You are among the hardest workers in the Zodiac. But when you take time out for recreation, as you should, you are satisfying a need that is very basic to your nature, and one that should not be denied.

You are happiest when you are creating something of beauty and of lasting value. For this reason, Taureans shine as gardeners. You are right at home when you plan and plant a garden. You will not only conceive it creatively, but care for it tenderly, so that it is indeed a "thing of beauty and a joy forever."

You Taureans are accomplished craftsmen. Whatever you turn out is finished perfectly in every detail. Many men of your sign can produce beautiful cabinetry and may make some of their own furniture. The women sew and knit well, and enjoy working with luxurious materials such as velvet, silk, angora.

They embroider and crochet well, and can make such articles
as beaded sweaters, embroidered tablecloths, perfectly. Because
they do not become easily bored, these women complete everything they begin.

Taureans are excellent hosts and hostesses. They are generous,
and serve "nothing but the best." A barbeque given by a native
of this sign is likely to be a long remembered occasion. They
enjoy not only hosting, but participating in cook-outs, beach
picnics, and so on. Theirs are the fullest hampers, filled with the
most delectable foods. In fact, cooking and baking are hobbies
that are very satisfying to these second-sign natives.

General Eisenhower, and former Prime Minister Churchill
helped to make amateur painting a popular hobby. It is one to
which you natives of Taurus take naturally. A set of oil paints,
and some canvas, or, if you want to begin in a less elaborate
manner, a box of water colors or pastels, can provide you with
endless hours of amusement. You will find you prefer to paint
still-life groupings, particularly those that feature flowers, or
landscapes, to portraits. In any event, you may amaze yourself
and your friends with your latent ability!

Another hobby that comes under the dominion of Taurus is
music. Many of you are talented, and are proficient at playing
an instrument. Others have good voices, and will enjoy such
activities as community sings and choirs. For those who do not
have the ability to create music, its enjoyment is just as satisfying. You are likely to have invested already in a hi-fi-set. Music
is likely to be an integral part of your life.

When it's vacation time for you, it is always something of a
problem to make plans. Basically you prefer your own home, and
all its comforts, to travel. You are not happy in strange places,
and feel self-conscious if you differ in your language and dress
from those around you. Furthermore, you are particular about
what you eat, prefering good, well-cooked food, on the rich side,
and plenty of it. You want your familiar surroundings and may
complain that you "can't sleep in a strange bed." For this
reason, it is sometimes wise for you to "vacation at home." You

may find that you have more fun gardening, doing some home-beautifying, and throwing a party or two, than you would if you spent the time away from home.

If you do take your vacation at a resort, or choose to travel, luxury is all-important to you. It is better for you to have a shorter holiday, than to try to make your vacation dollars stretch by "roughing it." You like to have some money in hand to buy souvenirs and gifts to bring back to your friends, so budget this item, too, when you make your vacation plans.

You enjoy the outdoors, and find much beauty in nature. Bird-watching, nature walks, hiking, are all of interest to you. Most of you do not enjoy competitive sport. Moreover, the women of this sign are likely to be afraid of anything that involves a risk to life or limb, such as skiing. At the beach, you would rather toast yourself in the sun, than swim. Peace and rest are more appealing to you than strenuous activity. However, if you do go in for athletics, you can become very accomplished, for if you are a typical Taurean, you have a strong, well-developed body, and good coordination.

Most important to you in your quest for relaxation is good fellowship. You feel that "old friends are best," and enjoy family outings, too. Not for you the search for new adventure. You are content in your own niche, finding fun and happiness in your own environment.

Gemini (May 22-June 21): As a Geminian, it is likely that you look forward all year to your vacations, and feel, when they are over, that they were all too short. You love change and adventure. Chameleon-like in your ability to adapt yourself to your surroundings, you are never afraid to travel to new places.

If you can possibly afford it, a trip abroad is something you should invest in. You might look into "travel now, pay later" plans that a travel agency may be able to offer you, if you cannot arrange the cash outlay. You will probably find that this sort of a vacation is worth any sacrifice you have to make.

You are an excellent traveler. You are equally happy in any

environment, so long as it is not the old familiar one! You can enjoy a sojourn in a hot climate, or a trip to the frozen north. And if you go anywhere in which your native tongue is not spoken, you find that in no time at all you have picked up enough of the new language to make yourself understood. Geminians are naturally linguistic.

Never be afraid to go anywhere by yourself, for loneliness is not going to be your problem. Wherever you go, you make friends. Amusing and interesting, you are sought-after company. And you have few prejudices, and so can accept people easily. Although you are choosy about your life companions, you have no objections to shipboard friendships and romances, for you accept the fact that they are temporary. You are always ready for a lark.

At home, you can find any number of activities in which you become engrossed. You have a rare ability to make good use of your leisure hours. You undoubtedly have a world of friends, and spend time entertaining. You are gifted as hosts and hostesses. Your parties and outings are characterized by the imagination that go into their planning. Elsa Maxwell, who is famous for planning society's most entertaining soirees, is a native of your sign. She once went so far as to enter a masquerade party riding an elephant! Without doubt, this is not a practical stunt for most of us, but it does indicate the spirit of fun that the Gemini natives have!

You, as a Geminian, can enjoy many diverse hobbies. You are facile with your hands, and can do beautiful work in any field in which manual dexterity is called for. You may enjoy making jewelry, for example, or leatherwork. A Geminian man we know has developed a hobby that is not only satisfying to him, but profitable, too. He makes tables with mosaic tops, and his designs are so lovely that he has a waiting list of people who want to buy them. Ceramics is another possibility. So is tatting, lacemaking, crocheting.

You are likely to have some writing or public speaking ability. A woman with Gemini prominent in her chart may take to doing publicity work for a volunteer organization. She is likely to be the editor of the P.T.A. Newsletter, for example. If she is secretary of her organization, she is sure to produce minutes that are not only concise and accurate, but even interesting, as well. To go a step further, many natives of this sign are talented at creative writing, and find the writing of stories, plays and poetry, an absorbing hobby.

You can excel at sports, if you wish, for you are nimble and quick. However, many of you do not have the patience to practice until you are really proficient. In games, you prefer speed. President Kennedy, a Geminian, plays a mean game of touch football, a fast, rugged sport. Hockey and tennis are often the choices of Gemini youngsters. Basketball is enjoyable for you, too.

In choosing your recreations, the most important consideration is that they provide a means of "getting away from it all." Unless you have an unusually exciting job, you find your daily routine often dull, and heartily enjoy any escapade in which you feel free. Yours is a blithe spirit, indeed, when you are out for fun and excitement!

Cancer (June 22-July 23): "Be it ever so humble, there's no place like home." Here is Cancer's sentiments to a "T." Your recreation, like every other part of your life, has home as its base. Although, occasionally, you feel that you may have a need for new scenery, you are always happiest when you return to your own hearth.

America is said to be the land where the goal of every family is not only two cars in the garage, but two homes—one a vacation refuge, as well. For members of your sign, this is an ideal way to live. You Cancerians would love to have a cabin in the woods, or even better, a cottage at the lake or seashore. You prefer to have your own belongings, and your familiar possessions, around you.

Yours is a water sign. Most of you Cancer natives like to be near the sea, if it is possible. You are keen on water sports, such as swimming, water-skiing, and particularly boating. You feel a sense of release when you are close to the water; the steady rhythm of the tides and the hum of the surf gives you a peace you rarely can attain anywhere else.

For this reason, if you do travel, you are likely to enjoy a cruise, or other trip in which you arrive at your destination by boat. You prefer warm climates to cool ones, and so a Florida or California vacation is a wise choice, as are trips to the Islands —Nassau, the Bahamas, Puerto Rico—if you can afford to go. Of course, if you are one of the lucky ones for whom a trip abroad is possible, you would enjoy a Mediterranean cruise very much.

However, by and large, most of your leisure time will probably be spent in your own backyard. It is there, by the way, that you like to entertain, too. Your sign rules food. Many a Cancerian man is handy with an outdoor grill, and the women like nothing better than setting up a picnic table loaded with delicious fare. Your kitchen, too, is a gathering place. "No matter where I seat my guests, they seem to like my kitchen best," reads a little sign in a Cancer woman's kitchen.

Your domestic nature also lends itself to hobbies. Besides fancy cooking, you may find relaxation in such hobbies as sewing for your home, renovation and do-it-yourself projects. Some members of your sign are expert at refinishing old furniture, turning a time-worn piece into a lovely accessory. You are patient and handy, and can happily spend hours sanding and removing old paint, before you apply a new finish.

In fact, antiques in general fascinate you. Collecting old glass and pewter is Cancer native Jacqueline Kennedy's hobby, and one that other members of this sign might take to. Other interests you may have are: old coins, stamps, even firearms. If your collection is one that can be displayed in your home, and is part of the decoration, so much the better!

There is another side to your nature, besides the one that inclines toward home and hospitality. You are rather mystical, and can get a lot of pleasure out of any hobby that concerns the supernatural. You are interested in ESP, for example, and other related fields. You enjoy reading about the supernatural; you may have quite a collection of science fiction books.

You have a need for solitude, too, to balance your lively home life. Reading, listening to music, are two occupations that you will find restful. You also enjoy nature very much, and are content to take a quiet walk to pick wild flowers.

With your sympathy and understanding of others, you are seldom at a loss for friends. People gravitate toward you, and you may find yourself involved in a more active social life than you wish. You are at your best with children. Any recreational work concerned with the small fry—scouting, boys and girls clubs, volunteer work in a children's ward at the hospital—is right up your alley. You have a great deal to give to children, and you receive deep satisfaction from time spent this way.

Leo (July 24-Aug. 23): As a native of this vital, zesty sign, you like to play as hard as you work. You have boundless enthusiasm, and can find an endless number of activities with which you can fill your leisure hours.

Yours is a nature that has little need for solitude. You do not require hours spent alone to replenish your energies, as do your Piscean or Cancerian brothers and sisters, for instance. Instead, you are at your best among groups of people. For that reason, vacations, hobbies and sports that provide you with an opportunity to be in congenial company, are the best for you.

If you are a typical Leo native, you enjoy luxury. Like your Taurus cousins, you would rather save for a really memorable vacation. A week or two at a plush resort hotel, for example, would satisfy your needs. You would enjoy a Florida vacation, or one in Las Vegas, or even the Islands or Hawaii. Wherever you go, it must be first-class. Cruises are fine for you; your attractive personality makes you a popular companion, and you soon are at the center of a social group.

You like excitement, and adore romance. A vacation at a spot that offers such activities as dancing under the stars, candle-light dinners, and so on, appeals to the romantic streak in your nature.

If you are a small town dweller, you might think about a trip to a large city, and a stay at a sophisticated hotel. You enjoy the glamour of the metropolis, the night life, the elegant shops,

and most of all, the theatres. You want to be waited on, and a
well-run hotel, in which you can enjoy such luxuries as breakfast in bed, for instance, would be a real treat.

Although you can have a good time at a winter resort where
you can ski and toboggan, and even take an old-fashioned ride
in a sleigh drawn by horses, a vacation in a warm place is
preferable. The Sun is your ruler, and you like to follow it. A
chance to loll under its rays (and acquire a tan that will be the
envy of your friends) is pleasant to you.

As for your leisure time at home, you have many avenues open
to you. It is a rare native of your sign who does not feel drawn
to the theatre in some way. Any recreation in which you have
a chance to satisfy your dramatic abilities, is a good choice. If
you have a little theatre group in your town, by all means, look
into it. If not, you might think about starting one. If actual
staging of shows is not feasible, you might consider starting a
play-reading group. Church and community service organizations
often plan pageants and plays as fund-raising devices.

Leo women enjoy any hobby in which they can vent their
artistic leanings. Interior decoration, designing and making their
own clothes or millinery, are good outlets. So is flower arranging.
Many a blue-ribbon at the garden show is taken by a Leo
woman.

You have a strong and sturdy body, and can excel at sports.
You prefer, of course, those in which you can cut something of
a figure. Sports such as water-skiing, and figure skating, are
enjoyable to you. You enjoy swimming, particularly if you can
show off a bit on the diving board. Like all the fire-sign natives,
you enjoy the excitement of danger, and love speed. Speedboats,
for instance, or racing cars appeal to you. By the way, many
members of your sign rather enjoy gambling, and trips to the
race track, for instance, might be a pleasant diversion to you.

As far as your friendships go, it need not be said again that
you are always popular and in demand. You love to go to
parties, and enjoy giving them. Your parties are characterized
by their lavishness, (for you are generous to a fault), and by
their dramatic themes. You might like to throw a party, with a

foreign theme—a Hawaiian luau, perhaps. At any rate, your home is likely to be a meeting place, for your entertaining is top-notch.

One of the problems Leo natives have is that when they become bored, they become lazy. Be sure that you do not allow yourself to get in a rut of hard work and responsibility, which will dull your appetite for pleasure. Make regular recreation a part of your life. You need it to retain your vitality.

Virgo (Aug. 24-Sept. 23): As a native of Virgo, you are more likely to have at least one thoroughly absorbing hobby, plus any number of other interests—more than those of any other members of the Zodiac, with the possible exception of Aquarius.

Yours is an exceptionally active mind. Everything around you is of interest to you. You are curious about your environment, and want to learn as much as you can. You enjoy so many diverse activities, that it is hard to find any subject that does not engage your attention at one time or another. For this reason, most of you are avid readers. You prefer non-fiction to fiction, generally. You are particularly fond of reading about controversial subjects. Your critical ability allows you to dissect and analyze the material and, thus you make well-founded decisions. Your opinions are sound, because you have taken the time to investigate thoroughly, and have carefully studied both sides of the picture.

You have a scientific turn of mind. You are likely to become a student of astrology, of anthropology, or of biology. In anything you do, you are extremely thorough. If you collect specimens, you not only make sure that you are exactly correct in your catologing, but you will search until you have even the rarest examples in your possession.

Most Virgoans are very handy. In fact, your do-it-yourself projects are truly professional. You can remodel your home, build or refinish furniture, with skill. The women of the sign are good needle-women, and can, if they set their minds to it, go in for as involved projects as upholstering and rugmaking. Here again, everything you turn out has a perfect finish.

You enjoy the simple life. Amusements such as working in

your garden, taking long walks, are pleasant to you. You have a certain need to be off by yourself, and can enjoy such solitary activities as hunting and fishing.

On your vacations, again, you are attracted by simplicity. Not for you the lush and expensive resorts. You can be content spending your summer holiday time in a cabin in the woods, where you are close to the nature you love.

Virgoans enjoy travel. They like to explore, to compare foreign ways with their own. On trips, they avoid the beaten path. They are curious about the living conditions in the various places they visit. However, travel presents certain hazards to them. For one thing, they are finicky about food, and cannot take exotic fare. They must have a plain diet, and meals at regular times. Then, too, cleanliness is very important to them. They are miserable if they cannot find immaculate lodgings. They cannot be comfortable in any place in which they are without plenty of hot, running water. Bathing and fresh clothing are very important to them, for they are fastidious people. Before they make travel arrangements, they must be sure that such facilities will be readily available to them.

As a Virgoan, you are nervous and active. Sports such as swimming, which offer you a chance to release your tensions, are very good for you. Because most of you tend to have rather confining jobs, you must be sure that you provide yourselves with recreation in which you have both change and relaxation. Fortunately, there are any number of outlets for you; and you are a rare Virgoan if you have not found many of them already!

Libra (Sept. 24-Oct. 23): You are a child of Venus, and so gaiety and pleasure come as naturally to you as breathing. You are a most unusual Libran if you have not found ways to fill your leisure time with fun. Members of your sign are rarely so tied down to their daily routine that they cannot find time for pleasure. The symbol of your sign is the scales, and you spend a lifetime seeking a balance in your life. You temper your work with play and your activities with rest.

The creation and appreciation of beauty is a part of your

life. You are likely to have some artistic hobby: painting, perhaps, at which you can excel, for you have a sure and perfect feeling for color and harmony. Many members of your sign are musical, and can either play an instrument, or sing, or have a fine understanding and appreciation of music. Most of you enjoy evenings at the opera, or in the symphony hall, or even just sitting at home and listening to fine records.

Like the natives of your sister sign, Taurus, the other Venusian section of the Zodiac, Librans tend toward hobbies in which beauty plays a part. If you are collectors, it will be of some delicate and lovely thing, such as porcelain. You love flowers, but dislike the arduous work that gardening requires. If you can have someone else do the laborious pruning and weeding, you can take a real pleasure in the beauty of your garden and fill your home with the loveliest blooms.

You are primarily a social creature. You prefer parties in which there are games and dancing. You simply love to get dressed up and go out, and dress up you do! You have exquisite taste, and love to plan and shop for your wardrobe. A Libra woman is likely to be the best-dressed gal in her crowd. Many women of your sign enjoy nothing more than a day spent in the stores, particularly the more expensive ones! Even window-shopping, if your budget is low, can provide a great deal of pleasure for you.

Your partner is most important in your scheme of things. You enjoy any activity in which you are part of a twosome. You enjoy sharing your interests, and like to talk things over. You enjoy club work, and generally become officers of any organization to which you belong. You make an excellent chairman, and a good committee member. Charity work appeals to you, but only if you do not come into contact with anything sordid. You can plan and execute a bazaar, or fund-raising party, for instance, but would not enjoy such occupations as visiting the patients in the hospital which your group benefits. You are a natural for such leisure time activities as civic beautification projects, for example, or the fund-raising committee for a new community center.

When you make your vacation plans, it is wise for you to select a spot in which you can be surrounded by congenial people. A lonely, remote place has little appeal for you. You are a delightful companion on a holiday; your happiness and exuberance are contagious. You are a good sport, and can take minor disappointments (which *do* crop up on vacations) in your stride. Yours is not a fault-finding personality. Wherever you go, you are liked. The "Ugly American" surely had no Libra planets in his charts! You are, in fact, the soul of charm and diplomacy. If you visit foreign lands, you are an excellent good-will ambassador.

Most Librans do not care for active sports. You have a good team spirit, and a fine sense of sportsmanship and fairness, but you do not often put them into use, for you do not enjoy strenuous athletic exercise. For one thing, you dislike getting messy and rumpled. You do not have much daring in your make-up, and anything that presents an element of physical danger is taboo for you. If you do go in for sports, it is likely to be some rather mild form.

One thing is certain: you do not have to be reminded that you must provide yourself with leisure time. You are already aware of this. If the demands of your home, or your business, are such that you are temporarily unable to find time to play, you make mental plans and happily anticipate the day you will be free to enjoy fun and recreation.

Scorpio (Oct. 24-Nov. 22): In everything you do, your play as well as your job, you put all your energies to work. You are among the most physically active people of the Zodiac. You must find an outlet for your athletic abilities. If you are typical of your sign, you are an excellent athlete. There is a good deal of daring in your make-up. You are not afraid of danger, in fact, you enjoy its challenge. Many famous mountain-climbers, for instance, have your sign strong in their charts.

You like rough-and-tumble sports. Football, soccer, hockey are good choices for the men of this sign. Anything competitive —tennis, squash, polo, basketball, badminton, for instance—is exciting to you. When you play, you play to win. If you lose, you may cover up your disappointment so that it is not noticed, but you are really only content to come in first.

You are a water-sign native, and like the natives of Pisces and Cancer, you are happy near the sea. You enjoy water sports, particularly boating and swimming. The water gives you a feeling of peace. If it is at all possible, you should plan on having a cottage near the ocean or a lake. Fishing, particularly of the deep sea variety, is a good outlet for you.

A sport that is Scorpio in nature, is skin-diving. This activity, which is rapidly gaining in popularity, combines the appeal of adventure and exploration, with the pleasures of the water, and has an unusual appeal for natives of your sign.

You enjoy any sort of exploration. You can adjust yourself to a simple existence, and can completely ignore a lack of creature comforts. You can be perfectly at home in the most primitive countries. You may dream of an African safari, for example, and know that if you are ever able to go on one, you will enjoy it fully. Like Robert Louis Stevenson, who left England, his home, for the exotic life on a primitive island, Adventure is your middle name!

Like other water-sign natives, you dislike throngs of people. You do not take well to strangers, and it takes you a long time to make friends. You treat new acquaintances with unfailing courtesy, but are somewhat distant. For this reason, club work is not your forte.

You need to be alone a great deal of the time. You find escape from your cares by retreating from society periodically. Give in to this need—it is essential to your happiness. Plan to have some time in which you can meditate, and some quiet recreations such as reading, or listening to music.

Most natives of your sign are fond of games of skill, such as cards, chess, checkers, anagrams, and on. You are likely to be an excellent card player. Shrewd and systematic, you thoroughly master any game you learn. You play a careful, "close to the vest" game, and are generally a winner! In chess, you can spend hours studying one game, and specialize in the more subtle aspects of it. Bridge and pinochle are interesting to you, too.

There is an occult side to your name. The study of astrology, for example, can provide you with many happy hours. You are drawn to metaphysics, in every form. You are intrigued by the mystery of the universe.

Although recreation is necessary for your well-being, as for everyone else, you may not make time for it. You may be so absorbed in your work—for you are singular in purpose—that it occupies your every waking hour. This is a grave mistake. Make it your business to plan for time for yourself, and do not skip your vacations.

Sagittarius (*Nov.* 23-*Dec.* 22): Giving advice to a Sagittarian about recreation is somewhat like telling Mickey Mantle where third base is! You are an expert on how to use leisure time. You have a rare ability to enjoy vacations and hobbies, and no matter how busy your life, you make sure that you have time for fun.

Sagittarius is the natural occupant of the ninth-house—the house of long distance travel, and of education and philosophy. It also has dominion over animals. Each of these categories works into your plan for recreation.

Travel is necessary to you. Although you may protest that you enjoy the comfort of your own home, you become bored and stultified in the same surroundings. You are a good traveler, and enjoy the trip, as well as the destination. You appreciate the beauties of nature. A trip to a national park, an automobile trip through New England to observe the beauties of the fall foliage, a journey that affords you a view of the lovely Blue Ridge mountains of the East, or the magnificent Rockies, is an excellent choice. You would enjoy a trip to Canada, for its rugged and majestic Laurentian mountains are indeed something to see.

Of course, a European trip, or one to the Orient, may be a life-long dream. Fortunately, in this day and age it is possible for many, many of us to travel abroad. Agencies offer excellent off-season rates, and group rates also make long-distance journeys possible. Travel is so interesting to you, and the appeal of far-away lands so strong, that many of you seek employment abroad. A note to Sagittarians who are free to live where they will—governmental agencies offer some interesting opportunities in overseas jobs, and you might find the slot you seek.

You are, by nature, inclined toward culture. Your intellectual interests are on a high level. You enjoy reading, and studying. If your community provides an adult education program at the local high school, college, or library, chances are you would enjoy taking some courses. If there are no such facilities available to you, you might form your own study group, by getting a group of friends together and hiring a teacher. The Great Books Course, offered by many libraries, or a course in a foreign language, would likely be most interesting to most members of your sign.

You enjoy the outdoors, for you feel free and unconfined when the sky is your roof. Hunting and horseback riding are favorites of many ninth-sign natives. Your sign rules animals, so any activity in which they are involved is usually fun for you. In fact, many of you derive a great deal of enjoyment from your pets, and may even breed them for a hobby. This is one hobby, by the way, that may be very profitable, too.

You enjoy sports. You like to play ball; you have good team spirit. You enjoy hiking, and can always find points of interest along the way. Any of the strenuous exercises are good for you. You are strong and vital, and you have a considerable amount of endurance. You like gymnastics, and are adept at this exercise. Like the other members of the fire-signs you are courageous, and a sport in which there is an element of danger is exciting to you.

Born under the beneficent influence of Jupiter, the planet of luck, you are lucky at games of chance. Many Sagittarian women like nothing more than playing Bingo, a game in which they find they win with surprising frequency. You may find card parties a very pleasant form of recreation, too. Sagittarian men enjoy "a night with the boys," and many belong to regular card groups.

You like people about you. You probably belong to at least one community group, or to a grange. Religion is a ninth-sign occupation. You may be one of the fortunate people who derive great happiness from his faith, but even if you are not really pious, you undoubtedly would enjoy church organizations and participating in the community programs they offer.

Capricorn (Dec. 23-Jan. 20): If you are a true Capricornian, you may need frequent reminders that recreation is as important in the scheme of things as is work and duty. You tend to skimp on your leisure time. The typical Capricornian woman, when she finds she has a few free hours, spends it straightening cabinets or laundering curtains, while the male of the species is likely to put in some overtime at his job!

Of course, this habit does not contribute to a well-balanced life. It is far wiser to delegate some time to play, than it is to allow your machine to run down from overwork. Far too many tenth-sign natives do not take their recreational needs into account until the need is pressing. No matter how enjoyable work is to you, there are surely some playtime activities that will prove interesting. It certainly is worthwhile to try a vacation for a change of scene, and a hobby or sport that provides a change of pace.

You are naturally a conservative person. You do not enjoy flashy surroundings or off-beat companions. On vacations, you like a solid, respectable resort, where you are more or less left to your own devices. If you find a suitable spot, you are content to return to it year after year. You do not enjoy any vacation situation in which you are forced to socialize with strangers. Although a man of this sign may have the reputation of being a "good fellow," he secretly prefers the company of his old friends and his family to that of new acquaintances.

It is probable that you do not care for travel. The women of the sign are inclined to be rather jittery about taking public conveyances, such as airplanes or ships. You enjoy your own table and your own bed, and do not want to "make do" when you are in less comfortable surroundings. You hate to be cramped by small cabins or berths. You are somewhat fussy about food, and exotic dishes do not agree with you.

In your choice of hobbies, there are many possibilities. Capricornians are great collectors. They like solid, tangible things, like coins and stamps. They are fascinated by history; many of them have historical collections, such as Civil War mementos, etc., They have a reverence for antiquity, and can derive a great deal of pleasure from hunting antiques.

Do-it-yourself projects, provided that they are far enough removed from your daily occupation, can be worthwhile leisure time activities. The results will be satisfying, too, for you are a neat and competent workman. Just be careful, again, that you do not become so intent on making home improvements that you work yourself ragged! You have a tendency to become engrossed in one interest, until it amounts to preoccupation.

Although you would be a real asset to any organization in which you became active, you are not likely to be a joiner. You have a lot to offer a church group, and can be an excellent civic worker. You take a responsible attitude toward such spare-time occupations as serving on school boards and library committees. If you are drafted into such a post, you may be surprised to learn that you really look forward to its meetings. Your opinions, though conventional, are thoroughly sound, and you become a most respected member of the group. This can be very satisfying to you, for you like nothing more than the feeling of fulfilling your responsibilities, and of being respected for it. Professional fraternities offer you an outlet, too. If you are a working woman, you might be interested, for instance, in the local business and professional women's club. Likewise, you enjoy alumni organizations, and can be the guiding spirit behind a class reunion.

You enjoy regulated fun. Being a member of a bowling team, or a card party group, for instance, can be a source of pleasure to you, provided you are well acquainted with all the other members.

For most of you Capricornians, the most pleasant occupation is a comfortable chair before your own fire, in the company of your dear friends or your family. This, to you, is rest and relaxation enough!

Aquarius (Jan. 21-Feb. 19): You are a native of the sign that rules the eleventh house of the Zodiac—the sign of friendship and fellowship, of clubs, organizations, and in fact, of humanity in the broadest sense. What does this mean to you, as an Aquarian? It means that you are likely to be well-acquainted with the pleasures of socializing, and that in all your activities, group interests are much in the forefront.

You are a joiner. You are more likely than not currently involved in so many worthwhile charitable and cultural organizations that the problem is how to make time for all of them. If you are not, you are denying your true nature. You need to work for a cause. Your convictions are deep. You are truly motivated toward the uplifting of your fellow man.

Such organizations as the Red Cross, hospital service groups, the Elks, the Masons, are in the dominion of Aquarius. You are an avid worker for any cause in which you believe, be it better schools, improved housing, medical care, disaster relief, and so on. You have a concept of a Utopian world—a world in which there is no hardship—and one way or another, it is toward this you work.

Your recreational pursuits are likely to be of much more interest to you than your job itself. You regret that you have so few leisure hours, for each of these is spent in pursuing an occupation that is dear to your heart.

You enjoy your hobbies, and you have many of them. You may be a photography buff, or pursue such interests as ceramics, painting, sewing, knitting, collecting, model-making, and so on. You enjoy doing things with your hands.

You are a good traveler. You prefer wide-open spaces to crowded cities. You derive a great feeling of peace and freedom while underway on the open road. A good choice for a vacation for you is the Northwest, particularly the Pacific states. You are very moved by nature's beauty, and can spend hours soaking up a beautiful view. The majesty of the mountains and the sea inspire you; and cause you to feel in harmony with your universe.

You are interested in foreign travel, and when you do visit a new place, you want to see how its people live. You do not restrict your visit to museum sightseeing, but instead find the by-ways and become familiar with the real life of the natives.

You have a cosmopolitan approach. You accept various folk-ways and mores as you find them, and are not shocked when you discover conditions other than those you had expected. There is nothing provincial in your make-up. And you are universally liked and accepted wherever you go, for your tolerance, your genuine feeling for your fellow man, are evident in your attitudes.

Cultural life appeals to you. You are interested in books, in music, in art, in the ballet. You enjoy lectures and readings. You are likely, at one time or another in your life, to take evening courses. History, geography, social studies, economics are prime subjects, for it is here that your interests lie.

As far as sports are concerned, you have a tendency to avoid the more strenuous types. You prefer hunting and fishing, or any activity that allows you a certain amount of communion with nature, to such organized sports as ball games, for instance. You are happier outdoors than in, and will be sure to find an avocation that permits you to spend time in the open air.

More than natives of other signs of the Zodiac, yours is one that bestows upon its natives a need to experience everything life has to offer. There is very little likelihood of your ever being in a rut—life is too varied and interesting to you for that. You want to express yourself fully, and to absorb within yourself everything about you. You will be sure that your leisure time is put to use, so that you can accomplish this goal.

Pisces (Feb. 20-March 21): For you, all life is a process of growth, and you are aware that you require certain stimuli in order to grow. You have a strong need for artistic expression, for companionship, and conversely, for solitude. It is these needs that can be satisfied through intelligent use of your leisure time.

Most natives of Pisces react keenly to their surroundings, and in fact, take on the coloration of their environment. That is why it is so important for you to spend as much time as you can in the company of those who can inspire and uplift you, and for you to avoid the sordid as much as possible.

You must be particularly careful in your choice of companions. It is easy for you to make friends, for your sympathy, your kindness, your gentleness are very appealing to others. In fact, there is a magnetic quality to natives of your sign, and people find it hard to resist them. But you must discriminate in your selections, and discourage the friendship of those who can only take from you. Do not allow yourself to become involved with people whose problems will drain you and depress you. Find, instead, friends who have an outgoing, happy approach to life, and with whom you can share wholesome activities.

Your need to be alone is one of the strongest facets of your personality. While you are among people you are, so to speak, constantly giving of yourself, and so you need time to reclaim yourself. You are given to meditation. You can spend many an evening completely by yourself, in calm contemplation. Do not deny yourself these hours by yourself.

If you are typical of your sign, you have strong artistic leanings. Your sign rules dancing. Women of this sign would enjoy a course in modern dance. If they can convince their husbands to participate in a series of ballroom dance lessons, it would be a lot of fun. Folk dancing is another possibility.

Music is very important to you; it helps you to relax your tensions. If you are like most natives of Pisces, you prefer romantic music to classical, and enjoy "mood music" particularly. If you have a feeling for it, you can derive a great deal of pleasure from playing an instrument.

Most of all, in your recreational pursuits, remember that your nature does not lend itself to a daily round of activities. Planned fun is torture for you. You need the leisure time to develop your own personality, to soul-search and find goals. You need to remove yourself, periodically, from your everyday cares and woes. You need to be alone to dream.

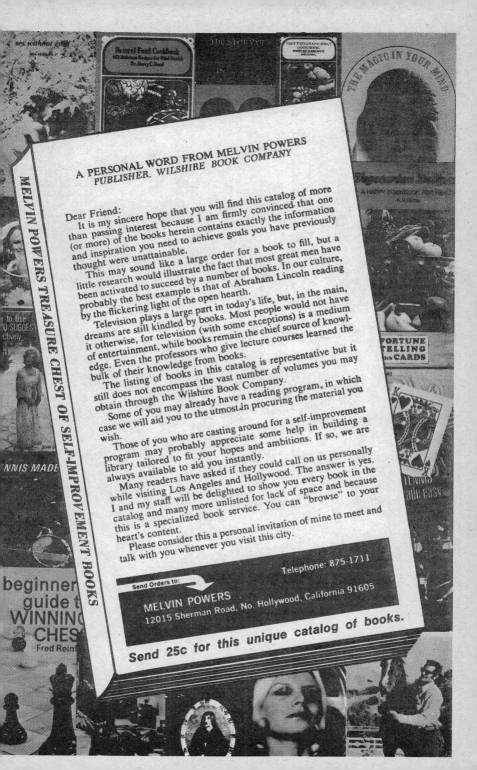

A PERSONAL WORD FROM MELVIN POWERS
PUBLISHER, WILSHIRE BOOK COMPANY

Dear Friend:

It is my sincere hope that you will find this catalog of more than passing interest because I am firmly convinced that one (or more) of the books herein contains exactly the information and inspiration you need to achieve goals you have previously thought were unattainable.

This may sound like a large order for a book to fill, but a little research would illustrate the fact that most great men have been activated to succeed by a number of books. In our culture, probably the best example is that of Abraham Lincoln reading by the flickering light of the open hearth.

Television plays a large part in today's life, but, in the main, dreams are still kindled by books. Most people would not have it otherwise, for television (with some exceptions) is a medium of entertainment, while books remain the chief source of knowledge. Even the professors who give lecture courses learned the bulk of their knowledge from books.

The listing of books in this catalog is representative but it still does not encompass the vast number of volumes you may obtain through the Wilshire Book Company.

Some of you may already have a reading program, in which case we will aid you to the utmost in procuring the material you wish.

Those of you who are casting around for a self-improvement program may probably appreciate some help in building a library tailored to fit your hopes and ambitions. If so, we are always available to aid you instantly.

Many readers have asked if they could call on us personally while visiting Los Angeles and Hollywood. The answer is yes. I and my staff will be delighted to show you every book in the catalog and many more unlisted for lack of space and because this is a specialized book service. You can "browse" to your heart's content.

Please consider this a personal invitation of mine to meet and talk with you whenever you visit this city.

Telephone: 875-1711

Send Orders to:

MELVIN POWERS
12015 Sherman Road, No. Hollywood, California 91605

Send 25c for this unique catalog of books.

Melvin Powers
SELF-IMPROVEMENT
LIBRARY

ASTROLOGY

_____ASTROLOGY: A FASCINATING HISTORY *P. Naylor*	2.00
_____ASTROLOGY: HOW TO CHART YOUR HOROSCOPE *Max Heindel*	2.00
_____ASTROLOGY: YOUR PERSONAL SUN-SIGN GUIDE *Beatrice Ryder*	2.00
_____ASTROLOGY FOR EVERYDAY LIVING *Janet Harris*	2.00
_____ASTROLOGY MADE EASY *Astarte*	2.00
_____ASTROLOGY MADE PRACTICAL *Alexandra Kayhle*	2.00
_____ASTROLOGY, ROMANCE, YOU AND THE STARS *Anthony Norvell*	3.00
_____MY WORLD OF ASTROLOGY *Sydney Omarr*	3.00
_____THOUGHT DIAL *Sydney Omarr*	2.00
_____ZODIAC REVEALED *Rupert Gleadow*	2.00

BRIDGE & POKER

_____ADVANCED POKER STRATEGY & WINNING PLAY *A. D. Livingston*	2.00
_____BRIDGE BIDDING MADE EASY *Edwin Kantar*	5.00
_____BRIDGE CONVENTIONS *Edwin Kantar*	4.00
_____COMPLETE DEFENSIVE BRIDGE PLAY *Edwin B. Kantar*	10.00
_____HOW TO IMPROVE YOUR BRIDGE *Alfred Sheinwold*	2.00
_____HOW TO WIN AT POKER *Terence Reese & Anthony T. Watkins*	2.00
_____SECRETS OF WINNING POKER *George S. Coffin*	3.00
_____TEST YOUR BRIDGE PLAY *Edwin B. Kantar*	3.00

BUSINESS STUDY & REFERENCE

_____CONVERSATION MADE EASY *Elliot Russell*	2.00
_____EXAM SECRET *Dennis B. Jackson*	2.00
_____FIX-IT BOOK *Arthur Symons*	2.00
_____HOW TO DEVELOP A BETTER SPEAKING VOICE *M. Hellier*	2.00
_____HOW TO MAKE A FORTUNE IN REAL ESTATE *Albert Winnikoff*	3.00
_____HOW TO MAKE MONEY IN REAL ESTATE *Stanley L. McMichael*	2.00
_____INCREASE YOUR LEARNING POWER *Geoffrey A. Dudley*	2.00
_____MAGIC OF NUMBERS *Robert Tocquet*	2.00
_____PRACTICAL GUIDE TO BETTER CONCENTRATION *Melvin Powers*	2.00
_____PRACTICAL GUIDE TO PUBLIC SPEAKING *Maurice Forley*	2.00
_____7 DAYS TO FASTER READING *William S. Schaill*	2.00
_____SONGWRITERS' RHYMING DICTIONARY *Jane Shaw Whitfield*	3.00
_____SPELLING MADE EASY *Lester D. Basch & Dr. Milton Finkelstein*	2.00
_____STUDENT'S GUIDE TO BETTER GRADES *J. A. Rickard*	2.00
_____TEST YOURSELF — Find Your Hidden Talent *Jack Shafer*	2.00
_____YOUR WILL & WHAT TO DO ABOUT IT *Attorney Samuel G. Kling*	2.00

CHESS & CHECKERS

_____BEGINNER'S GUIDE TO WINNING CHESS *Fred Reinfeld*	2.00
_____BETTER CHESS — How to Play *Fred Reinfeld*	2.00
_____CHECKERS MADE EASY *Tom Wiswell*	2.00
_____CHESS IN TEN EASY LESSONS *Larry Evans*	2.00
_____CHESS MADE EASY *Milton L. Hanauer*	2.00
_____CHESS MASTERY — A New Approach *Fred Reinfeld*	2.00
_____CHESS PROBLEMS FOR BEGINNERS *edited by Fred Reinfeld*	2.00
_____CHESS SECRETS REVEALED *Fred Reinfeld*	2.00

Melvin Powers
SELF-IMPROVEMENT
LIBRARY

SEW SIMPLY, SEW RIGHT *Mini Rhea & F. Leighton*   2.00
STAMP COLLECTING FOR BEGINNERS *Burton Hobson*   2.00
STAMP COLLECTING FOR FUN & PROFIT *Frank Cetin*   2.00

HORSE PLAYERS' WINNING GUIDES

BETTING HORSES TO WIN   *Les Conklin*   2.00
HOW TO PICK WINNING HORSES   *Bob McKnight*   2.00
HOW TO WIN AT THE RACES   *Sam (The Genius) Lewin*   2.00
HOW YOU CAN BEAT THE RACES   *Jack Kavanagh*   2.00
MAKING MONEY AT THE RACES   *David Barr*   2.00
PAYDAY AT THE RACES   *Les Conklin*   2.00
SMART HANDICAPPING MADE EASY   *William Bauman*   2.00

HUMOR

BILL BALLANCE HANDBOOK OF NIFTY MOVES   *Bill Ballance*   3.00
HOW TO BE A COMEDIAN FOR FUN & PROFIT   *King & Laufer*   2.00

HYPNOTISM

ADVANCED TECHNIQUES OF HYPNOSIS *Melvin Powers*   1.00
CHILDBIRTH WITH HYPNOSIS *William S. Kroger, M.D.*   2.00
HOW TO SOLVE YOUR SEX PROBLEMS
     WITH SELF-HYPNOSIS *Frank S. Caprio, M.D.*   2.00
HOW TO STOP SMOKING THRU SELF-HYPNOSIS *Leslie M. LeCron*   2.00
HOW TO USE AUTO-SUGGESTION EFFECTIVELY *John Duckworth*   2.00
HOW YOU CAN BOWL BETTER USING SELF-HYPNOSIS *Jack Heise*   2.00
HOW YOU CAN PLAY BETTER GOLF USING SELF-HYPNOSIS *Heise*   2.00
HYPNOSIS AND SELF-HYPNOSIS *Bernard Hollander, M.D.*   2.00
HYPNOTISM *(Originally published in 1893) Carl Sextus*   3.00
HYPNOTISM & PSYCHIC PHENOMENA *Simeon Edmunds*   2.00
HYPNOTISM MADE EASY *Dr. Ralph Winn*   2.00
HYPNOTISM MADE PRACTICAL *Louis Orton*   2.00
HYPNOTISM REVEALED *Melvin Powers*   1.00
HYPNOTISM TODAY *Leslie LeCron & Jean Bordeaux, Ph.D.*   2.00
MODERN HYPNOSIS *Lesley Kuhn & Salvatore Russo, Ph.D.*   3.00
NEW CONCEPTS OF HYPNOSIS *Bernard C. Gindes, M.D.*   3.00
POST-HYPNOTIC INSTRUCTIONS *Arnold Furst*   2.00
     How to give post-hypnotic suggestions for therapeutic purposes.
PRACTICAL GUIDE TO SELF-HYPNOSIS *Melvin Powers*   2.00
PRACTICAL HYPNOTISM *Philip Magonet, M.D.*   2.00
SECRETS OF HYPNOTISM *S. J. Van Pelt, M.D.*   2.00
SELF-HYPNOSIS *Paul Adams*   2.00
SELF-HYPNOSIS Its Theory, Technique & Application *Melvin Powers*   2.00
SELF-HYPNOSIS A Conditioned-Response Technique *Laurance Sparks*   3.00
THERAPY THROUGH HYPNOSIS *edited by Raphael H. Rhodes*   3.00

JUDAICA

HOW TO LIVE A RICHER & FULLER LIFE *Rabbi Edgar F. Magnin*   2.00
MODERN ISRAEL *Lily Edelman*   2.00
OUR JEWISH HERITAGE *Rabbi Alfred Wolf & Joseph Gaer*   2.00
ROMANCE OF HASSIDISM *Jacob S. Minkin*   2.50
SERVICE OF THE HEART *Evelyn Garfield, Ph.D.*   3.00
STORY OF ISRAEL IN COINS *Jean & Maurice Gould*   2.00
STORY OF ISRAEL IN STAMPS *Maxim & Gabriel Shamir*   1.00
TONGUE OF THE PROPHETS *Robert St. John*   3.00
TREASURY OF COMFORT *edited by Rabbi Sidney Greenberg*   3.00

MARRIAGE, SEX & PARENTHOOD

ABILITY TO LOVE   *Dr. Allan Fromme*   3.00
ENCYCLOPEDIA OF MODERN SEX & LOVE TECHNIQUES *Macandrew*   3.00
GUIDE TO SUCCESSFUL MARRIAGE *Drs. Albert Ellis & Robert Harper*   3.00
HOW TO RAISE AN EMOTIONALLY HEALTHY, HAPPY CHILD, *A. Ellis*   2.00
IMPOTENCE & FRIGIDITY *Edwin W. Hirsch, M.D.*   2.00
NEW APPROACHES TO SEX IN MARRIAGE *John E. Eichenlaub, M.D.*   2.00
SEX WITHOUT GUILT *Albert Ellis, Ph.D.*   2.00

_____ SEXUALLY ADEQUATE FEMALE *Frank S. Caprio, M.D.*   2.00
_____ SEXUALLY ADEQUATE MALE *Frank S. Caprio, M.D.*   2.00
_____ YOUR FIRST YEAR OF MARRIAGE   *Dr. Tom McGinnis*   2.00

METAPHYSICS & OCCULT

_____ BOOK OF TALISMANS, AMULETS & ZODIACAL GEMS *William Pavitt*   3.00
_____ CONCENTRATION—A Guide to Mental Mastery *Mouni Sadhu*   3.00
_____ DREAMS & OMENS REVEALED *Fred Gettings*   2.00
_____ EXTRASENSORY PERCEPTION *Simeon Edmunds*   2.00
_____ FORTUNE TELLING WITH CARDS *P. Foli*   2.00
_____ HANDWRITING ANALYSIS MADE EASY *John Marley*   2.00
_____ HANDWRITING TELLS *Nadya Olyanova*   3.00
_____ HOW TO UNDERSTAND YOUR DREAMS *Geoffrey A. Dudley*   2.00
_____ ILLUSTRATED YOGA *William Zorn*   2.00
_____ IN DAYS OF GREAT PEACE *Mouni Sadhu*   2.00
_____ KING SOLOMON'S TEMPLE IN THE MASONIC TRADITION *Alex Horne*   5.00
_____ MAGICIAN — His training and work *W. E. Butler*   2.00
_____ MEDITATION *Mouni Sadhu*   3.00
_____ MODERN NUMEROLOGY *Morris C. Goodman*   2.00
_____ NUMEROLOGY—ITS FACTS AND SECRETS *Ariel Yvon Taylor*   2.00
_____ PALMISTRY MADE EASY *Fred Gettings*   2.00
_____ PALMISTRY MADE PRACTICAL *Elizabeth Daniels Squire*   3.00
_____ PALMISTRY SECRETS REVEALED *Henry Frith*   2.00
_____ PRACTICAL YOGA *Ernest Wood*   3.00
_____ PROPHECY IN OUR TIME *Martin Ebon*   2.50
_____ PSYCHOLOGY OF HANDWRITING *Nadya Olyanova*   2.00
_____ SEEING INTO THE FUTURE *Harvey Day*   2.00
_____ SUPERSTITION — Are you superstitious? *Eric Maple*   2.00
_____ TAROT *Mouni Sadhu*   4.00
_____ TAROT OF THE BOHEMIANS *Papus*   3.00
_____ TEST YOUR ESP *Martin Ebon*   2.00
_____ WAYS TO SELF-REALIZATION *Mouni Sadhu*   2.00
_____ WITCHCRAFT, MAGIC & OCCULTISM—A Fascinating History *W. B. Crow*   3.00
_____ WITCHCRAFT — THE SIXTH SENSE *Justine Glass*   2.00
_____ WORLD OF PSYCHIC RESEARCH *Hereward Carrington*   2.00
_____ YOU CAN ANALYZE HANDWRITING *Robert Holder*   2.00

SELF-HELP & INSPIRATIONAL

_____ CYBERNETICS WITHIN US *Y. Saparina*   3.00
_____ DAILY POWER FOR JOYFUL LIVING *Dr. Donald Curtis*   2.00
_____ DOCTOR PSYCHO-CYBERNETICS *Maxwell Maltz, M.D.*   3.00
_____ DYNAMIC THINKING *Melvin Powers*   1.00
_____ GREATEST POWER IN THE UNIVERSE *U. S. Andersen*   4.00
_____ GROW RICH WHILE YOU SLEEP *Ben Sweetland*   2.00
_____ GROWTH THROUGH REASON *Albert Ellis, Ph.D.*   3.00
_____ GUIDE TO DEVELOPING YOUR POTENTIAL *Herbert A. Otto, Ph.D.*   3.00
_____ GUIDE TO LIVING IN BALANCE *Frank S. Caprio, M.D.*   2.00
_____ GUIDE TO RATIONAL LIVING *Albert Ellis, Ph.D. & R. Harper, Ph.D.*   3.00
_____ HELPING YOURSELF WITH APPLIED PSYCHOLOGY *R. Henderson*   2.00
_____ HELPING YOURSELF WITH PSYCHIATRY *Frank S. Caprio, M.D.*   2.00
_____ HOW TO ATTRACT GOOD LUCK *A. H. Z. Carr*   2.00
_____ HOW TO CONTROL YOUR DESTINY *Norvell*   2.00
_____ HOW TO DEVELOP A WINNING PERSONALITY *Martin Panzer*   3.00
_____ HOW TO DEVELOP AN EXCEPTIONAL MEMORY *Young & Gibson*   3.00
_____ HOW TO OVERCOME YOUR FEARS *M. P. Leahy, M.D.*   2.00
_____ HOW YOU CAN HAVE CONFIDENCE AND POWER *Les Giblin*   2.00
_____ HUMAN PROBLEMS & HOW TO SOLVE THEM *Dr. Donald Curtis*   2.00
_____ I CAN *Ben Sweetland*   3.00
_____ I WILL *Ben Sweetland*   2.00
_____ LEFT-HANDED PEOPLE *Michael Barsley*   3.00
_____ MAGIC IN YOUR MIND *U. S. Andersen*   3.00
_____ MAGIC OF THINKING BIG *Dr. David J. Schwartz*   2.00

MAGIC POWER OF YOUR MIND *Walter M. Germain*   3.00
MENTAL POWER THRU SLEEP SUGGESTION *Melvin Powers*   1.00
ORIENTAL SECRETS OF GRACEFUL LIVING *Boye De Mente*   1.00
OUR TROUBLED SELVES *Dr. Allan Fromme*   3.00
PRACTICAL GUIDE TO SUCCESS & POPULARITY *C. W. Bailey*   2.00
PSYCHO-CYBERNETICS *Maxwell Maltz, M.D.*   2.00
SCIENCE OF MIND IN DAILY LIVING *Dr. Donald Curtis*   2.00
SECRET OF SECRETS *U. S. Andersen*   3.00
STUTTERING AND WHAT YOU CAN DO ABOUT IT *W. Johnson, Ph.D.*   2.00
SUCCESS-CYBERNETICS *U. S. Andersen*   3.00
10 DAYS TO A GREAT NEW LIFE *William E. Edwards*   2.00
THINK AND GROW RICH *Napoleon Hill*   3.00
THREE MAGIC WORDS *U. S. Andersen*   3.00
TREASURY OF THE ART OF LIVING *Sidney S. Greenberg*   3.00
YOU ARE NOT THE TARGET *Laura Huxley*   3.00
YOUR SUBCONSCIOUS POWER *Charles M. Simmons*   3.00
YOUR THOUGHTS CAN CHANGE YOUR LIFE *Dr. Donald Curtis*   2.00

SPORTS

ARCHERY — An Expert's Guide *Don Stamp*   2.00
BICYCLING FOR FUN AND GOOD HEALTH *Kenneth E. Luther*   2.00
CAMPING-OUT 101 Ideas & Activities *Bruno Knobel*   2.00
COMPLETE GUIDE TO FISHING *Vlad Evanoff*   2.00
HOW TO WIN AT POCKET BILLIARDS *Edward D. Knuchell*   3.00
MOTORCYCLING FOR BEGINNERS *I. G. Edmonds*   2.00
PRACTICAL BOATING *W. S. Kals*   3.00
SECRET OF BOWLING STRIKES *Dawson Taylor*   2.00
SECRET OF PERFECT PUTTING *Horton Smith & Dawson Taylor*   2.00
SECRET WHY FISH BITE *James Westman*   2.00
SKIER'S POCKET BOOK *Otti Wiedman* (4¼" x 6")   2.50
SOCCER—The game & how to play it *Gary Rosenthal*   2.00
TABLE TENNIS MADE EASY *Johnny Leach*   2.00

TENNIS LOVERS' LIBRARY

BEGINNER'S GUIDE TO WINNING TENNIS *Helen Hull Jacobs*   2.00
HOW TO BEAT BETTER TENNIS PLAYERS *Loring Fiske*   3.00
HOW TO IMPROVE YOUR TENNIS—Style, Strategy & Analysis *C. Wilson*   2.00
PLAY TENNIS WITH ROSEWALL *Ken Rosewall*   2.00
PSYCH YOURSELF TO BETTER TENNIS *Dr. Walter A. Luszki*   2.00
TENNIS FOR BEGINNERS *Dr. H. A. Murray*   2.00
TENNIS MADE EASY *Joel Brecheen*   2.00
WEEKEND TENNIS—How to have fun & win at the same time *Bill Talbert*   2.00

WILSHIRE MINIATURE LIBRARY (4¼" x 6" in full color)

BUTTERFLIES   2.50
INTRODUCTION TO MINERALS   2.50
LIPIZZANERS & THE SPANISH RIDING SCHOOL   2.50
PRECIOUS STONES AND PEARLS   2.50
SKIER'S POCKET BOOK   2.50

WILSHIRE PET LIBRARY

DOG OBEDIENCE TRAINING *Gust Kessopulos*   2.00
DOG TRAINING MADE EASY & FUN *John W. Kellogg*   2.00
HOW TO BRING UP YOUR PET DOG *Kurt Unkelbach*   2.00
HOW TO RAISE & TRAIN YOUR PUPPY *Jeff Griffen*   2.00
PIGEONS: HOW TO RAISE & TRAIN THEM *William H. Allen, Jr.*   2.00

The books listed above can be obtained from your book dealer or directly from
Melvin Powers. When ordering, please remit 25c per book postage & handling.
Send 25c for our illustrated catalog of self-improvement books.

Melvin Powers

12015 Sherman Road, No. Hollywood, California 91605

NOTES

NOTES